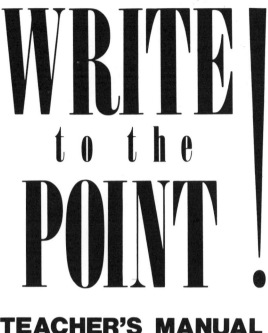

WRITE to the POINT !

TEACHER'S MANUAL

William P. Morgan

National Textbook Company
a division of *NTC Publishing Group*

Contents

Teaching Suggestions   **1**

Application and Sequence   1

Structure of the Student's Text   1

Schedule   2

Grades   3

Evaluation of Essays   3

    Sample Evaluation Sheet 1   4

    Sample Evaluation Sheet 2   4

    Sample Evaluation Sheet 3   5

    Sample Evaluation Sheet 4   6

Reducing the Paper Load   7

The First Day   9

Outside Reading   10

    Outside Reading Plan (assignment form)   10

    Outside Reading Plan (student reporting form)   11

Vocabulary   12

Notebooks   12

Keeping a Journal   13

Essay Files   13

Word Processing   13

Revision   13

    Peer Evaluation Form   14

    Revision Form   15

Publishing Student Writing   16

Selected Readings   **17**

Chapter 1: The Persuasive Edge   **19**

Instructional Objectives   19

Vocabulary   19

Motivation   19

Don't Be Afraid of Grammar   19

Make Plans   20

Use a Thesis Sentence   22

Support Your Idea   22

Be Specific   23

Chapter 2: The Alpha and the Omega   **25**

Instructional Objectives   25

Vocabulary   25

Motivation   25

Introductions   26

Conclusions   27
The Whole Essay   27

Chapter 3: Improvement Is the New Goal   **30**
Instructional Objectives   30
Vocabulary   30
Motivation   30
Some Don'ts and Some Do's   31
Eliminate Unnecessary Information   32
Eliminate Unnecessary Words   33
Keep It Simple   34
Using Transitions   35

Chapter 4: Finding Your Writing Voice   **36**
Instructional Objectives   36
Vocabulary   36
Motivation   36
Be Yourself, Only Better   36
Use Active Verbs   37
Use Short, Varied Sentences   38
Remember Your Readers   39
Checklist for Writers   40

Chapter 5: Cause and Effect   **41**
Instructional Objectives   41
Vocabulary   41
Motivation   41
A Real-life Application   42
Four Guides to Basic Organization   43
Three Traps to Avoid   44
The Parts and the Whole   45

Chapter 6: Definition   **47**
Instructional Objectives   47
Vocabulary   47
Motivation   47
Abstract and Concrete Language   48
Scale of Abstraction   49
Types of Definition   49
Methods of Extended Definition   50
Writing a Definition Essay   51

Chapter 7: The Classification Essay   **53**
Instructional Objectives   53
Vocabulary   53
Motivation   53

The Mind Needs Order   54
Classification in Your Writing   55
Preparing to Write   56
Developing Your Essay   57
A Whole Essay   57

Chapter 8: Comparison and Contrast   **59**
Instructional Objectives   59
Vocabulary   59
Motivation   59
Comparison or Contrast?   60
The Thesis Statement   61
Organization   61
A Comparison and Contrast Essay   62

Chapter 9: The Inductive Argument   **65**
Instructional Objectives   65
Vocabulary   65
Motivation   65
Arguing Inductively   67
Reliability of Inductive Reasoning   68
Gathering Your Own Evidence   69

Chapter 10: Refutation   **71**
Instructional Objectives   71
Vocabulary   71
Motivation   71
Examine Background and Evidence   71
Examine the Logic   73
Structure Your Refutation   75

Chapter 11: The Research Paper   **77**
Instructional Objectives   77
Vocabulary   77
Motivation   77
Focusing on a Subject   78
Gathering Resources   79
Reading and Taking Notes   80
Writing the First Draft   80
Revising the First Draft   81
Preparing the Final Copy   81

TEACHING SUGGESTIONS

In any school, the most demanding teaching assignment is composition. Aside from the typically overwhelming reading load that comes with the job, the major difficulty is that writing is a skill that must be practiced and developed. Your students arrive that first day of class with individual differences, aptitudes, and attitudes that could mystify the most talented and organized of teachers. A course outline that worked beautifully with last year's class may be a dismal failure with your newest group of students.

In spite of the fact that lesson plans are best left in the hands of the individual classroom teacher or a departmental committee that knows the needs of the students involved, the overworked teacher of composition may appreciate a few concise suggestions.

Application and Sequence

Write to the Point! is recommended as the basis for a one-semester, college preparatory composition course, or for the composition portion of a full-year, advanced language arts course.

It may be used in the order you find most effective, but the author's intention is that the first four chapters should serve as a foundation for the rest of the text. Studying each chapter in order will be appropriate for most students, but if special circumstances suggest another approach, trust your own training, experience, and professional judgment.

Many teachers of college preparatory composition courses would save a unit on persuasive writing for the end of the course, the theory being that the student could then put to use all the forms—definition, classification, comparison and contrast, cause and effect—that have been practiced earlier. This text, however, is based on two premises: (1) in the sense that writers want readers to share their opinions, almost all essay writing is persuasive, and (2) students will develop strength in their writing from the sense of structure and discipline learned in persuasive writing. The text then builds on that discipline and structure with additional forms and specific purposes.

Whatever the specific writing task, when the writer creates a thesis and selects and organizes information to support that thesis, his or her writing has a built-in advantage— purpose and organization.

Structure of the Student's Text

Write to the Point! contains several features to help students develop and master writing skills.

- The Checklist for Writers is used at key points in the text to highlight essential information. When appropriate, the Checklist simplifies, organizes, and stresses ideas that the students can use to develop essential skills. For instance, one Checklist presents questions the writer can answer to develop effective description. At other times, it provides students with step-by-step guides to lead them through various writing tasks. An example is the Checklist that leads the student writer through three steps to writing an introduction.

1

- The Section Summaries condense pages of material into one or two paragraphs that can be used to easily review basic concepts. The summaries will help students retain what they have learned, and you can use them to point out the most essential information of each section.

- Student-written compositions are used to model every major writing assignment, and discussion questions lead students through an analysis of each of those compositions. The questions point out strengths and weaknesses in the essays, and invite students to consider alternative approaches that could have been used.

Schedule

The amount of time you devote to each chapter of *Write to the Point!* will depend on the needs of your class and the amount of supplementary material you choose to bring into the class. A tentative schedule for a one semester course might look like this:

Chapter 1. The Persuasive Edge		
2. The Alpha and the Omega		
3. Improvement Is the New Goal	}	3 weeks
4. Finding Your Writing Voice		
5. Cause and Effect		2 weeks
6. Definition		"
7. The Classification Essay		"
8. Comparison and Contrast		"
9. The Inductive Argument		"
10. Refutation		"
11. The Research Paper		3 weeks
Total		**18 weeks**

Of course, many variations are possible. Depending on your class, you may decide to spend two weeks or four weeks on Chapters 1 through 4. The research paper may require four weeks of class time. The number of days spent on Chapters 5 through 10 can be adjusted to accommodate whatever changes you think necessary. The time periods suggested, however, have been tested and found reasonable for most students.

The student is asked to write a major essay at the end of Chapter 2 and for each of Chapters 5 through 10. The following sample schedule, adjusted to meet the needs of your class, could be used with each of those chapters.

Day 1. Begin new unit with introductory discussion, assignment of vocabulary list, and reading.

2. Discussion, vocabulary, and activities.

3. Discussion, vocabulary, and activities.

4. Essay assignment and brainstorming activities.

5. Students write a thesis statement, an outline, and a plan for development of essay. Share and discuss in class.

6. Teacher returns essays from previous chapter and discusses them privately with students. Students make necessary revisions.

7, 8, 9. Writing laboratory. First draft will be due on day 7 or 8. Teacher will be conducting informal conferences with students. Students should be exploring ideas, sketching, planning, drafting, reading, reflecting, revising, and sharing with other students. The number of days devoted to these activities can be adjusted to meet the needs of your class, but three seems minimal.

10. Unit test. Final copy of essay will be due on the following day.

Grades

Assigning grades is never easy, and when you are dealing with material as subjective as a student's writing, the responsibility becomes even more onerous. Students will appreciate it, and your job will be easier, if you tell them ahead of time how grades will be assigned. Grades will probably result from evaluation of essays, quizzes, unit tests, homework assignments, class participation, and the use of independent work time in class. Consider the following scale as a starting point, and adjust it to fit your own situation.

Major essays	approximately 60%
Quizzes, tests, and homework	approximately 25%
Class participation and use of independent work time	approximately 15%

Evaluation of Essays

Evaluation of major essays will be easier and more productive if you develop an evaluation sheet that allows you to judge each essay on specific criteria as well as make marginal comments to the student.

The following sample evaluation sheets can be adapted to your own requirements. You may choose to use ideas from several to create the evaluation sheet that works best for you and your class.

Sample Evaluation Sheet 1

Student _____

Assignment _____

Date _____

	Excellent	Good	Fair	Poor	Unsatisfactory
Organization					
Purpose					
Material					
Expression					
Mechanics					

Final Score _____

Sample Evaluation Sheet 2

Student _____

Assignment _____

Date _____

	5	4	3	2	1
Introduction					
Thesis					
Topic sentences					
Conclusion					
Persuasiveness					
Expression					
Organization					
Sentence variety					
Mechanics					

Total Evaluation _____

Sample Evaluation Sheet 3

Student _____

Assignment _____

Date _____

Above Average .... **Needs Improvement**

	5	**4**	**3**	**2**	**1**
Introduction					
Thesis					
Support 1					
Support 2					
Support 3					
Additional Support?					
Conclusion					
Organization					

Comments:

Total Points Received _____

Sample Evaluation Sheet 4

Student _____ Assignment _____ Date _____

1. Purpose (10%)   Your Points _____
   A. Clear, well-narrowed thesis
   B. Language, tone appropriate
   C. Body of essay stays on topic
   D. Body of essay fully develops thesis
   E. Shows awareness of reader

2. Supporting Evidence (30%)   Your Points _____
   A. Topic sentences clearly stated
   B. Topic sentences clearly related to thesis
   C. Use concrete details (quantity, quality)
   D. Complete explanations
   E. Independent ideas

3. Organization (15%)   Your Points _____
   A. Effective introduction
   B. Well structured paragraphs
   C. Logical progression of ideas
   D. Clear transitions
   E. Effective conclusion

4. Expression (15%)   Your Points _____
   A. Concise language
   B. Logical, unambiguous sentences
   C. Variety of sentence structures
   D. Accurate and appropriate word choice
   E. Appropriate level of formality

5. Writing Process (15%)   Your Points _____
   A. Exploring ideas
   B. Outlining, note taking, planning
   C. Time spent drafting
   D. Revising at all levels (words, sentences, paragraphs)
   E. Sees revising as ongoing process

6. Mechanics and Usage (15%)   Your Points _____
One error per 100 words is the minimum standard. In practice this means there
will be a 1% penalty for each error.
Total points possible   _____
Total points earned   _____
Points deducted for lateness _____

Final Score _____

Reducing the Paper Load

As a typical English teacher, you probably meet with 125 or more students every day. Each time your classes hand in a major essay, you face an unenviable task. Giving the work of each of those 125 students just ten minutes of your time, you will need almost 21 hours to evaluate their writing—unless you add a ten-minute break for a cup of coffee.

Add the hours necessary for checking daily assignments, reading journals, correcting tests, and trying to keep up with professional reading, and you have what seems like an impossible job. If you are going to survive, you need to be as efficient as possible. Here are some suggestions for giving yourself the time to evaluate papers thoroughly when it is necessary.

1. You do not have to read everything each student writes. Much of a student's work is preliminary and is not intended to be read by you or anyone else. You may be able to help at several points in the writing process, but the student does not need your reaction to every step. And, at some times, peer reaction may be both more effective and more efficient.

2. Use student revision groups. Besides giving you more time, peer revision offers several advantages to the student writer. For too many students, the teacher is the only audience they have ever written for and, as a teacher, you are not a typical audience. The opinions of their peers are very important to students; as a result, the writer who is going to be critiqued is highly motivated.

   Peer revision also offers benefits to those students reading others' work. They will see several different ways an assignment can be handled and are certain to exchange methods for developing ideas and dealing with organization. Here are some suggestions for organizing student revision groups.

   a. Limit the groups to three or four students.

   b. Demonstrate the kinds of response students should give each other. It may be worthwhile to lead a class discussion on the kinds of response that students think they would find most helpful.

   c. All students must be treated with respect. The way you model the demonstration of proper responses will go a long way toward avoiding problems.

   d. As students become more comfortable with the idea of sharing their work with others, they will conduct their own informal peer revision conferences. Encourage the practice. If students form their own groups, the results will almost always be positive.

   e. Unless a group of students does not work well together, maintain the same groups through several writing assignments so they become more comfortable with each other. If some groups do not work well together, rearrange them. Some groups may have too great a variety of writers, and some groups just waste time. Either situation justifies a change.

3. You do not have to evaluate all writing the same way. For example, if the purpose of an assignment is for students to write an essay in which they develop and explain their own views about an abstract idea, you might restrict your comments to how well a student uses different methods of definition.

4. You can do much of the reading in class before the papers are completed. If you conduct your class as a writing laboratory or workshop, you will already be very familiar with the students' work and, while the essays you are evaluating will be much more polished, you will be able to read and comment quickly and effectively.

5. You can preface your evaluation with a student's self-evaluation. This is not self-evaluation in the sense that the student determines his or her own grade, but a method of letting you know where the student is most likely to need direction. Prepare a form that is appropriate for the assignment. Questions such as the following ask the student to make specific comments about his or her paper.

   a. What do you think are the strongest points of this paper? Why? What part do you like best? Why?

   b. Where do you still feel dissatisfied about this paper? Why? What part gave you the most difficulty? Why?

   c. Would you like me to make suggestions for rewording any part of this paper? If so, circle that section and write ''RW?'' in the margin.

   d. In the process of writing, you probably considered putting some things into this paper and later changed your mind. What did you leave out? Why?

   e. What did you learn from writing this paper? Indicate anything new you tried to accomplish with this assignment.

6. You can use student proofreading groups. Having students proofread each others' papers offers several advantages besides reducing the time you need to point out mechanical problems. You may have heard yourself say, ''I never learned _____ so well as when I had to teach it.'' By encouraging students to explain the errors they find, you put them in the role of teacher, and they will remember the ideas they discuss. Students will get into arguments and raise questions of usage that never arise when they depend on the teacher to find usage problems. Have students use the proofreading symbols at the end of *Write to the Point!*

7. You can schedule a conference with each student. Strictly speaking, this may not save you a lot of time, but it won't take longer than writing comments on the paper. And it will be much more effective because you can ask questions of the student and discuss the essay rather than just react to it.

   Your own schedule will determine how easily and how often you can schedule conferences with each student, but it is very important that the student have a chance to discuss his or her work with you. Even if you have to use class time to do so, try to schedule several conferences during the year.

The First Day

You have undoubtedly found that classes do not get off to a good start when you plan a long lecture for the first day. There is always enough official, beginning-of-the-semester busywork to fill fifteen or twenty minutes of class time. That comes very close to filling the average student's listening quota for one class period. Use the remaining time for an activity that engages the students' minds and teaches them a useful skill.

Brainstorming is an exceptionally effective method for stimulating creative thinking and producing new ideas. Your students should be given two or three practice sessions sometime during the first few weeks of class. The first day of class would be a good opportunity to start.

Since this is very likely an early experience with brainstorming, limit discussion to factual topics so that there is no temptation to get sidetracked by differences of opinion. Pick one of the following topics and ask the students to suggest everything they can think of that would be appropriate material for:

- Describing baseball—"What aspects of the game should be included in a complete description of baseball?"

- Describing a current event—"What significant facts should be mentioned if you want someone to understand _____?"

- Describing the uses to which the United States government puts tax money— "What programs, activities, and needs do our tax dollars support?"

For this activity, you should act as recorder, but have the students jot down the information for themselves so they will have a record if you run out of time or space. At the chalkboard or on an overhead projector, write down everything mentioned, even suggestions that you recognize as weak ones. Poor ideas may lead to worthwhile ones if the mind is allowed to roam freely. Make the point that, when brainstorming, one delays judgments until after all the possibilities have been exhausted.

When students have suggested all they can, ask them to suggest ways to group the material you have recorded. Do not settle for the first arrangement, even though it will likely be a reasonable one. The point is to examine different options so students can make the best choices. Continue to act as recorder, arranging and rearranging the notes. Also, if students come up with additional ideas, be sure to add these to the original list.

As the third step, ask students to write a one-sentence statement of the main point they would want to make if they actually wrote a paper on this topic. Each student should draft his or her own sentence. Read several of them aloud. Choose one, or combine the best elements of several statements, and write the resulting sentence on the chalkboard.

You may want to finish by discussing which items from the original list the students might want to drop after considering their statement of the main point. Because the students may later think of new relationships that could suggest additional possibilities, even the rejected ideas should not be erased. Cross them out, but do not erase anything.

Students will recognize the value of letting their minds soar. Throughout the course, take time for brainstorming when the opportunity arises. There will be many occasions when students need the advantage of free association to fill the gaps in their thinking. "Let's see if we can think of some ideas that would help Jenni with her essay" will not only help Jenni but also give the class valuable practice in producing useful ideas.

Outside Reading

Students can learn a good deal about writing when they read articles of opinion from current newspapers and magazines. Also, if you set up a schedule requiring one outside reading per week, by the time they need a research topic or are looking for opinions to refute at the end of Chapter 10, students will have plenty of material to draw from.

It is also a good idea to focus the students' reading by having them choose, at the beginning of the semester, several general topics for investigation. For instance, a student may decide that he or she wants to learn what professional writers are saying about an international question, the Supreme Court, or new uses of computers in education. The student's list might expand later, but developing a specific reading plan will help keep the assignment from becoming a random, last-minute chore completed sloppily. You may want to make one of the first homework assignments a list of five or six topics each student wants to read about during the semester. The following form can be used to keep track of progress.

Outside Reading Plan

NAME _____   DATE _____

	Title	**Magazine**	**Date**

Topic 1: _____

    1st article:
    2nd article:
    3nd article:

Topic 2: _____

    1st article:
    2nd article:
    3nd article:

Topic 3: _____

    1st article:
    2nd article:
    3nd article:

Topic 4: _____

       1st article:
       2nd article:
       3nd article:

Topic 5: _____

       1st article:
       2nd article:
       3nd article:

Make the form as long as you like.

Show students how to use the *Readers' Guide to Periodical Literature* to find articles on their topics. Assign a specific time each week when the assignment will be due, and supply students with a form like the following.

OUTSIDE READING

NAME _____

DATE _____

1. Magazine

2. Title of article

3. Author

4. Number of pages

5. Publication date

6. Subject

Answer all questions in full sentences.

1. What is the author's opinion about the subject? Be specific.

2. What arguments, or reasons, did the author use to try to persuade the reader to his or her point of view?

3. How do you feel about the arguments you found in this article? Do you agree, disagree, or both? Did anything in the article change your mind on the subject? Did you learn anything new?

Vocabulary

Keep a standard-sized dictionary on your desk and use it often. If you must move from room to room for classes, the effort of including the dictionary among the paraphernalia you carry around will be repaid by the example it sets for your students. Students need to see that you were not born with the vocabulary you now use. They need to see that a useful, effective vocabulary, an ease with words, can be developed and that the goal is important enough to justify the effort.

Students will benefit from regular, formal vocabulary work. List the words supplied with each chapter of this book on the chalkboard the first day of each unit. Set a date when students will be responsible for knowing and being able to use the new terms. You can handle the mechanics of this assignment in several ways, but students should at least be required to record definitions and write sentences in their notebooks illustrating the use of each word.

Spend four or five minutes at the beginning of each period discussing vocabulary words. It is a good activity for getting students into the right frame of mind for the day's work, and they will be receptive if you make the time profitable for them. Discuss difficulties they may be having with their vocabulary assignment and demonstrate the context in which some of the words are commonly used. Talk about the connotations associated with the words and ask for sample sentences. Students will find it helpful, and you will be better able to keep track of their progress. Don't be concerned with the fact that some students might be able to escape looking up a few words. You will be discussing the most difficult examples and going well beyond the kind of information they are likely to find in a standard dictionary. If students are truly unfamiliar with a word, the dictionary definition is seldom enough to allow them to use the word effectively in their writing.

Students can be held responsible for new words in several ways. A quiz near the end of the unit will tell you how effective their study has been, and it is reasonable to include the vocabulary in unit tests. As the semester progresses, do not hesitate to retest words from earlier vocabulary lessons.

Notebooks

Ask students to keep their notes and assignments in a notebook reserved for this class. Ideally, students should use a three-ring binder so that pages can be added or removed at will. Notes can be organized and reorganized, as needed, and pages devoted to such things as vocabulary, brainstorming exercises, or mechanical problems can be kept separate from notes on units studied or essays written. The notebook should include summaries of important information from the text, notes from the teacher's instructions, useful ideas from class discussion, explanations to clarify technical problems a student may have, and any other material that might be useful.

To encourage students to develop a good note-taking system, you might want to give credit for particularly well done notebooks at the end of each grading period.

Keeping a Journal

Most students enjoy writing in their journals. Encourage it by using all the journal topics in *Write to the Point!* and by supplying a few minutes two or three times a week for students to add to their journals. Do everything you can, including writing in your own journal, to encourage students to make the journal a habit. The practice of filling a page on a regular basis, without the pressure of formal assignments, can do a lot to make students more comfortable with the idea of writing. It can also be a source of ideas for later use.

Collect and read students' journals about once a month. Don't make it a time-consuming task. Skim to spot interesting topics and make one or two comments. Don't note mechanical errors or assign grades. Student writers can express themselves much more freely when the threat of a grade is removed, and it is appropriate for the journal to be as free from pressure as possible. If students want a portion of their writing to remain private, using the three-ring binder and loose-leaf paper should make it easy for them to withhold a page.

Essay Files

Keep student essays in a file set aside for the purpose. This allows you to go back and note the progress made by students throughout the course. It also encourages students to see their work as more meaningful than a paper that will be graded, returned, and thrown away. In addition, particularly well written essays can be used as models for future students.

Word Processing

Word processors are more and more available for students, and their effectiveness in teaching writing is well documented. If word processors are available in your building, you may want to take class time for an introduction to their use. You may even want to offer extra credit for students who can produce typed final copies of their essays. Considering the degree to which word processing encourages students to revise their work, a 2- to 5-percent bonus added to major essay grades would not be unreasonable.

Don't discourage students from using programs that check spelling. Their greatest advantage is as proofreading tools, and students still need to be aware of homophones.

Revision

Ideally, students would think of revision as occurring on many levels. Chapters 3 and 4 of *Write to the Point!* encourage the attitude that, while revising for correctness is good, revising for effective communication is much more important. It would be a good idea to try to keep the two—correctness and communication—separate.

As much as possible, encourage a great deal of revision for effective communication during the classroom writing laboratory sessions. You should be reading students' early drafts, asking pertinent questions, and making suggestions for improvement so that students can do a great deal of revising before making a formal copy of the essay. This will also make your final evaluation much easier and less time-consuming because you will already be familiar with each student's paper. Require that early drafts be written and available in class at least a couple of days before the due date so that students do not fall into the habit of wasting class time and then writing their essays the night before the final copy is due. If necessary, assign a portion of the essay's grade to work done on the first and second drafts.

Students can also help each other by reading, questioning, and making suggestions. Encourage sharing of early drafts so that students have the benefit of an audience while they are writing. (For suggestions on setting up peer revision groups, see Reducing the Paper Load earlier in this manual.)

If your students are reluctant to share their work with each other informally, attach four or five copies of the following peer evaluation form to each student's work. Hand the papers to students randomly, telling them to read the essay, answer the questions, and pass the essay on to another student. Keep the process as informal and nonthreatening as possible.

Peer Evaluation Form

What do you like about my essay?

What don't you understand about my essay?

If you would be willing to talk to me about my essay, sign your name.

You may want students to resubmit papers for a higher grade. If so, you can emphasize the difference between correctness and content, and lighten your own reading load, by creating a correction sheet that asks students to rewrite only those sentences that have technical problems. Insist that students write the whole sentence. When the problem has been resolved, you might want to add to the student's grade about half the points that were originally lost because of mechanical errors. Use the following form, or make one that fits your own objectives. Students can use more than one form if necessary.

Whatever format you use, set a strict time limit for mechanical revisions. One week should usually be plenty. Otherwise, some students will remember only when they face the prospect of a poor grade at the end of the semester. Then you will face dozens of hurriedly completed, poorly done revisions that benefit the student very little.

Revision Form

Name _____ Essay # _____

Number of mechanical errors on this essay _____

Error 1: _____.

Correction: _____.

Error 2: _____.

Correction: _____.

Error 3: _____.

Correction: _____.

Error 4: _____.

Correction: _____.

Error 5: _____.

Correction: _____.

Error 6: _____.

Correction: _____.

Error 7: _____.

Correction: _____.

Error 8: _____.

Correction: _____.

Error 9: _____.

Correction: _____.

Error 10: _____.

Correction: _____.

Publishing Student Writing

Any activity that broadens a student's audience is worth pursuing. While the opportunities for actually publishing may be limited, you can do several things that will distribute student writing beyond the classroom.

1. Display particularly good work on an English department bulletin board.

2. Exchange completed essays with another class.

3. Have students write for a real audience and send their work to that audience. Parents, local politicians, business people, leaders of civic organizations, and school administators can all be targeted. Encourage recipients to respond to the student writing.

4. Collect student writing in large loose-leaf notebooks and make them available for other students to read.

Nothing motivates writing like the possibility of publication, and there are several things you can do to promote students' work.

1. School newspapers often print letters to the editor. Many class assignments can be made appropriate for that use.

2. Your school newspaper can print student class work in a special edition. This, of course, could include work from creative writing classes.

3. Most school districts publish a newsletter that goes to students' parents. Student work could be included.

4. Many communities have a "shopper's newspaper" that consists mostly of classified advertisements. Perhaps the editor would consider printing a few pieces of
   student work as attention-getters.

5. Ask the editor of your local newspaper to establish an opinion page guest column
   for high school readers.

6. Establish a central location for contest announcments and information about student literary magazines.

7. Subscribe to writers' magazines.

8. Help students learn to use *Writer's Market* and submit their work in the proper
   manuscript format.

9. Establish a file of published work that can be used as models.

SELECTED READINGS

Atwell, Nancie. *In the Middle: Writing, Reading, and Learning with Adolescents.* Portsmouth,
   N.H.: Boynton/Cook Publishers, 1987. Atwell teaches eighth-grade students, but her techniques are applicable to all levels. Four chapters on establishing a writing workshop are particularly interesting.

Elbow, Peter. *Embracing Contraries.* New York: Oxford University Press, 1986. Not a collection of activities for the classroom, this is, rather, a collection of Elbow's essays on the nature
   of teaching and learning. Written from his own experience, the book encourages teachers to
   be more inventive.

_____. *Writing Without Teachers.* New York: Oxford University Press, 1973. Elbow popu-
   larized the technique of freewriting to generate and develop ideas. The title refers to his belief
   that teachers should become writers with their students.

Fulwiler, Toby, ed. *The Journal Book.* Portsmouth, N.H.: Boynton/Cook Publishers, 1987. A
   collection of essays by teachers of all grade levels from elementary to college. Filled with
   ideas that can be adapted to high school and junior college, the book has a large section devoted to using the journal as a teaching device.

Kirby, Dan, and Tom Liner. *Inside Out.* Portsmouth, N.H.: Boynton/Cook Publishers, 1981.
   Practical information for the composition teacher. Chapters on classroom environment, the
   use of journals, responding to student writing, and grading are especially interesting.

Knapp, Linda Roehrig. *The Word Processor and the Writing Teacher.* Englewood Cliffs, N.J.:
   Prentice-Hall, 1986. A useful text both for teachers who use word processing every day and
   for teachers who have never seen a word processor but want to begin a program. The book
   covers everything from defining word processing to producing student publications.

Laque, Carol Feiser, and Phyllis A. Sherwood. *A Laboratory Approach to Writing.* Urbana, Ill.:
   NCTE, 1977. Offering strategies, models, and exercises for all stages of the writing process,
   the book is especially useful for developing an individualized approach to teaching writing.
   The authors' experiences are in high school and college freshman composition courses.

Lindemann, Erika. *A Rhetoric for Writing Teachers.* New York: Oxford University Press, 1987. Covers all aspects of teaching writing. Chapter 6, Prewriting Techniques, is particularly interesting.

Murray, Donald. *Expecting the Unexpected.* Portsmouth, N.H.: Boynton/Cook Publishers, 1989. A collection of Murray's previously published articles, inspired by his own classroom experience, the book tells teachers to welcome the unexpected, to reward student spontaneity.

_____. *A Writer Teaches Writing: A Practical Method of Teaching Composition.* Boston: Houghton Mifflin, 1968. Murray provides practical suggestions from his classroom while discussing the writing process.

Solomon, Gwen. *Teaching Writing with Computers.* Englewood Cliffs, N.J.: Prentice-Hall, 1986. Applies computer technology to many writing forms. Solomon presents a convincing argument for using word processing in the classroom for what she calls the POWER process. POWER is an acronym for Prewrite, Organize, Write, Exchange, and Revise.

Chapter 1
The Persuasive Edge

Instructional Objectives

As a result of having studied this chapter, students will

1. consider their audience and purpose before writing

2. learn to gather and organize information for an essay

3. write thesis statements for their essays

4. write topic sentences and paragraphs of support for their thesis statements

5. write a photographic paragraph.

Vocabulary

Put the vocabulary words on the chalkboard and, if possible, leave them there for the duration of this chapter. Students should learn to spell, define, and use in a sentence each of the following terms:

circumvent	decorum	deplore	vapid
antipathy	invective	astute	petulant
accrued	pseudo	turgid	dilatory
consummate	coterie	torpor	truculent
beguile	mundane	flaccid	palpitate

Motivation

Before students start the chapter, discuss the kinds of difficulties they have had with writing. Ask what kinds of problems bother them most and what, if any, aspects of writing they feel comfortable with. Point out that most tasks are made easier with a system—a procedure—to follow. People read directions to assemble an audio system, follow coaching instructions to improve athletic ability, and consult maps to drive across the country. Following that principle, students are going to be learning some specific steps that will make writing easier than it might have been in the past.

Don't Be Afraid of Grammar

Discuss

1. To what degree . . . your writing? Explain.

   Correctness is important because it can affect both meaning and the impression a reader gets of the writer. Most students, however, do not have to be overly concerned about clarity of meaning. They need to be concerned about such things as spelling, punctuation, and verb and pronoun forms, and all of these can be aided by finding the right kind of help.

2. What steps can . . . English usage skills?

Most students' usage skills can be improved by a conscious effort to use the aids available. A spelling dictionary, a usage manual, and reliable proofreaders help enormously. More important than anything else are a positive attitude and an effort to write as clearly as possible.

3. What is the . . . to this purpose?

The main purpose of writing is communication. Clarity and correctness are extremely important. If writing can be interpreted more than one way, or if problems of correctness make the writer look unreliable, the reader will not be concentrating on the writer's message.

Be sure students understand that, while clarity is of prime importance, a lack of correctness can also seriously undermine the writer's message. Problems with correctness should not keep the student from writing, but neither should those problems be ignored.

Act

1. Answer each of . . . any general statements.

The questions are intended to encourage a self-examination on the part of the student. Secondarily, they should give you a chance to become better acquainted with the students and learn more about their writing and attitudes toward writing.

2. Look through some . . . both versions together.

Students need to begin developing the idea that a first draft is seldom perfect. Do not be overly critical, but encourage them to look at their writing with a fresh eye and an open mind.

3. Talk to several . . . your work occasionally.

Some of these proofreaders will be more helpful than others, but insist on a list of specific people who can contribute their skills. Encourage students to find proofreaders who come from a variety of backgrounds and age groups.

Make Plans

Discuss

1. What equipment should . . . you are writing?

The writer obviously needs paper and pen, but several other tools are helpful. Research notes, a dictionary, a thesaurus, and a spelling dictionary should be close at hand.

2. Describe the process . . . be while brainstorming?

Brainstorming is the process of encouraging a spontaneous flow of ideas. In this case, the writer is looking for ideas that will accomplish the goal of his or her writing.

Order, relative importance, and persuasiveness are not as important as getting a large number of ideas down on paper. Stress the point that students should not take time to judge the usefulness of these ideas. Making judgments slows down or discourages the flow. At this point, the quantity of ideas is much more important than quality.

If you have not been able to practice brainstorming with the class, as discussed in the Teaching Suggestions section of this manual, now is a good time to demonstrate. Ask the class, "How many reasons can you think of to support the idea that teenagers need their own cars?" Encourage them to suggest a large number of reasons, not just the ones they think are the best or the most acceptable. Be sure they understand that limiting answers at this point may keep them from thinking of some of the most imaginative and most convincing reasons.

3. What questions might . . . about a subject?

How, why, and *when* questions generate the kinds of ideas the writer needs at this point.

4. What is the . . . by your brainstorming?

The purpose of brainstorming is to allow the mind to come up with the best list of ideas possible. It initially produces a large amount of material, probably much more than the writer needs. It also produces ideas of varying importance. Its strength lies in the fact that, among that large number of ideas, the writer will usually think of some excellent ones that he or she might have otherwise overlooked.

Selecting, dropping, and clustering are merely the first steps in arranging those ideas into the most effective form possible.

Act

1. Make a list . . . not yet written.

Insist that students think in terms of individuals or specific groups. Discourage answers such as "a general audience" or "anyone interested in sports." It is important that they picture a specific audience.

2. Pick three of . . . be your purpose?

Students must narrow the general topic to a purpose, a more specific topic, that can be handled within a reasonable length.

3. Choose one of . . . they do it?"

The question calls for developing ideas that will eventually be used as support for the essay's thesis. Have small groups of students, two or three, work together and arrive at a consensus.

4. Look at your list . . . to put them?

Through clustering their ideas, students should be able to imagine the parts of an essay falling into place. Some will need help at this point. Encourage students to share their answers and stress the fact that ideas may be correctly grouped many ways.

Use a Thesis Sentence

Discuss

1. What are the . . . a thesis sentence?

The thesis states in a single sentence the opinion being expressed in your essay. When you write a thesis sentence, the need to explain your opinion creates a specific purpose for the essay. Additionally, the evidence needed to support the thesis gives the essay an organizational pattern.

2. List the six . . . is so important.
   a. The thesis should be a full sentence.
   b. The thesis should be a declarative sentence rather than a question.
   c. The thesis should state only one major idea.
   d. The thesis should state that idea with certainty.
   e. The thesis should be expressed in precise language.
   f. The thesis should immediately suggest a clear and meaningful idea.

Use discussion of why each characteristic is important to emphasize the fact that the thesis must be absolutely clear in the writer's mind and be expressed in language that is both clear and concise.

Act

In this activity, students may benefit from working through all the steps together.

1. Name one topic . . . a definite opinion.

Warn students that they should feel informed enough about this topic to be able to explain themselves fully.

2. If necessary, narrow . . . five hundred words.

Most students' original topics will be too broad for an essay of only five hundred words. To some students, writing five hundred words may sound impossible, and they will resist narrowing the topic. Don't dismiss their concerns, but point out that five hundred words is less than the average newspaper opinion column, and they will be explaining all of their reasons for feeling the way they do.

3. Keeping in mind . . . really believe in.

The two previous questions worked together to give the students practice in creating a thesis statement that expresses an honest, supportable opinion. After each student has read his or her thesis statement, you may find it useful to ask for specific reasons for feeling that way. Don't press the issue, but get them thinking about the fact that expressing an opinion creates the responsibility of supporting that idea.

Support Your Idea

Discuss

1. Why is it . . . support their opinions?

When you make a statement of opinion, it is natural for others to wonder why you feel that way. If you have good reasons for your ideas, readers or listeners can be convinced to change their minds.

2. To what degree . . . good as another's?

An opinion is only as worthwhile as the reasons supporting it. If a writer cannot say why he or she feels a certain way, the reader is not going to take the opinion seriously and will certainly not be convinced.

3. What form should . . . your thesis take?

The support for your thesis should come in the form of topic sentences and a paragraph of explanation for each topic sentence.

4. What process can . . . support your thesis?

Answer the magic-word questions from Section 2, Make Plans. "How?" "How do you know that?" "Why?" "Why is that true?" "Why do you say so?"

5. After writing topic . . . your supporting paragraphs?

Use the same questioning technique that produced the topic sentences. *How* and *why* work well, but there are other possibilities as well. "In what way is this true?" "When is this true?" "Where is this true?" "What makes this happen?"

Act

Again, students may benefit from working together on this activity. You may choose to have them develop this outline as a group project, brainstorming ideas together, or you may simply allow them to assist each other even though each student is required to develop his or her own ideas. Either way, it is important that students begin to feel comfortable exchanging ideas, exploring possibilities, and examining the topic thoroughly before actually writing.

1. Look back in . . . tuition tax credits.

Be sure students understand that the purpose here is to practice expressing themselves clearly. Whatever their opinions, they should be capable of making a precise statement and clearly supporting that statement.

2. Name one topic . . . one of the following:

Remind students to narrow the topic enough so that it can be treated in an essay of about five hundred words. They should also be familiar enough with this topic to be able to explain themselves.

3. Using this thesis . . . three topic sentences.

If students have problems writing topic sentences, remind them to ask, "*How* do you know that?" "*Why* is that true?" Developing the habit of always asking *how* and *why* will make developing topic sentences automatic.

4. The goal of . . . to develop it.

Remind students that when they complete this step—writing questions they would ask about each topic sentence and the answers to those questions—they will have an outline of their planned essay.

Be Specific

Discuss

1. What is the . . . about student writing?

The most common complaint is that support is not specific enough. Be sure to hold students accountable for specific details and explanations in their writing. It is important that they consider content as even more important than form.

2. What is the . . . about a man''?

Ideas, abstractions, are difficult to write about, and even more difficult for the reader to follow. ''Humankind'' is not an easy concept to picture. On the other hand, a specific human being—John Wayne, Kim Basinger, or the student's boyfriend or girlfriend—is easier to picture and discuss.

3. How can you . . . *talented* or *ambitious?*

Find, or create, an example that illustrates the idea you have in mind. Describe that example in such detail that the reader can picture almost exactly the same person or scene.

4. What kinds of . . . to think about?

Details, such as location, relationship between parts of the scene, size, color, movement, feeling, sound, smell, and taste, make the example easier for the reader to understand and appreciate.

Act

At the end . . . how it is true.

This is, of course, a descriptive paragraph. Insist that students take the few moments necessary to imagine details they can use, jot them down, and select the best ones. They should start out with more specific details than they actually need.

This is also a good time to begin sharing their writing. Begin by having one of the more confident writers read to the class and ask the students who are listening to tell which details of description they think did the best job of getting the picture across. At this time, all comments should be positive ones.

Chapter 2
The Alpha and the Omega

Instructional Objectives

As a result of having studied this chapter, students will

1. learn six methods of introducing an essay

2. practice essay introductions

3. learn four guidelines governing the use of conclusions

4. learn five methods of concluding an essay

5. practice essay conclusions

6. read and evaluate a persuasive essay

7. write a persuasive essay.

Vocabulary

Put the vocabulary words on the chalkboard and, if possible, leave them there for the duration of this chapter.

curtail	alleviate	gird	inclement
mandatory	supersede	insinuate	caprice
doldrums	verbatim	soliloquy	ludicrous
clientele	exhilaration	refute	covenant
charlatan	chaos	homogeneous	chafe

Motivation

On the day before beginning this chapter, bring to class two or three essays that have particularly interesting introductions. Weekly newsmagazines are a good source of professionally written persuasive writing. *Newsweek,* for instance, publishes a column called "My Turn," an opinion essay of about 1,000 words written by the magazine's readers. You can either photocopy the essays or put them on an overhead projector; it is important that students be able to see what you are talking about.

Ask students to look through a few magazines and newspapers of their own for additional essays of opinion that have what they think are interesting openings. Each student should be able to find and bring to class at least one essay with the introduction circled. Have a few students read their introductions to the class, and post the collection on the bulletin board for reference as students work on their own introductions.

Introductions

Discuss

1. Why might it . . . of the essay?

If you write the introduction first, you probably have an incomplete idea of what you are introducing. Very likely, you aren't even certain how long the essay will be. When the body of the paper is complete, you will find it easier to think of an *appropriate* way to lead into the thesis.

2. What is the . . . it is used.

The generic introduction imitates the method people use in conversation when they want to bring up a subject without being too obvious about their intentions. The writer chooses one word or idea from the thesis and makes a comment about that word or idea. The writer then continues with related thoughts to develop a paragraph about the topic, all the while leading the discussion toward the thesis statement itself.

3. Name and describe five specialized introductions.

   a. Quotations: Repeat the opinion of some well-known person.

   b. Personal Experiences: Tell about an incident that reminds you of the topic.

   c. Famous Person Anecdote: Tell a story about an experience involving a well-known person.

   d. Questions: Ask a rhetorical question involving the topic.

   e. Refutations: Discuss your opposition's main argument and show how it is wrong.

4. How can you . . . for an introduction?

Normally, the introduction should be no more than 15 to 20 percent of the whole essay. Be sure students understand that this is a guideline only. Special circumstances could lead a writer to make the introduction either longer or shorter. For instance, a particularly interesting Famous Person Anecdote could take longer to tell, or an appropriate quotation might result in a relatively short introduction.

Act

Read the following . . . some of your own.

Any writing activity will be more effective if the students write about topics they are interested in. In Chapter 1 students wrote practice thesis sentences. The text supplies sample thesis sentences for those students who need them, but this activity will be much easier and more realistic if they use their own thesis sentences from Chapter 1.

Since students have not yet written a complete essay, tell them to assume the essay they are introducing is about 500 words long. When the introductions are completed, have students read them aloud. Ask each to explain why that method of introduction seems most appropriate for his or her thesis.

Conclusions

Discuss

1. List and explain . . . use of conclusions.
   a. The conclusion should be relevant, clear, and concise.
   b. The conclusion should be a full paragraph with its own topic sentence.
   c. The topic sentence of the conclusion should be an imaginative reminder or rewording of the thesis.
   d. The conclusion should have a purpose beyond marking the end of the essay. It should make a point.
2. Name the five . . . might be appropriate.
   a. Recommendations are particularly effective if the essay has been critical of a situation.
   b. Predictions are effective when the essay is about a situation with possibly far-reaching consequences.
   c. Calls to action are effective if the essay is about a continuing problem that needs to be dealt with, possibly by the reader.
   d. Stimulating quotes are effective if the topic has also been discussed by well-known, highly respected people.
   e. Summaries are effective when the essay is long or complex. A summary should be avoided, however, unless it is likely to make keeping facts straight easier for the reader.

   You might ask students to add example of specific topics with which the different types of conclusions would work well. For instance, "If an essay has been critical of your town's lack of weekend activities for teenagers, it might be a good idea to conclude by recommending what should be done about the situation."

Act

Look back at . . . conclusion for each.

Insist that students use the same topics for which they wrote introductions in the previous Act. (see page 31). Afterwards, ask them to explain the advantages of the method of conclusion they used.

The Whole Essay

Discuss

1. Identify the thesis . . . thesis sentence answering?

   The thesis is, "Legalizing marijuana would be a tragic mistake for our society."

   The thesis answers the question, "Is legalizing marijuana a good way of solving the problems of drug abuse and the crime that accompanies that abuse?"

2. List the supporting . . . the thesis statement?

The supporting points are:

a. "If marijuana became legal, drug use would begin at an earlier age."

b. "In addition to children using drugs, law-abiding adults might begin sampling legalized marijuana."

c. "The addiction rate among drug users would increase."

d. "Last, the lives of innocent people would be greatly endangered if marijuana became legal."

Each of the supporting points answers the question, "How, or in what way, would legalizing marijuana be a tragic mistake for our society?"

3. Choose two of . . . by the topic sentence.

Students will be able to intelligently judge the support given in the essay if you insist that they be specific with their praise or criticism. You might ask, "Could the writer have given more specific examples? Where?"

4. Which type of introduction . . . might work here?

This essay uses a generic introduction, bringing up the topic of our legal system's failure to control people's behavior and the fact that people often suggest solving the problem by legalizing the behavior. The writer then gets more specific by giving drug use as an example.

Any of the introduction forms might have worked as well, but students are likely to suggest quoting a well-known person, telling about a personal experience or observation, or asking a question about the topic of drug abuse. Ask for an example of how each could be used. Students may not think of a quotation immediately, but they can tell about television shows they have seen, recount stories about entertainment industry personalities or famous athletes who have had their careers cut short by drug use, or ask a question that leads into the topic of legalizing marijuana.

5. What type of conclusion . . . might work well?

The essay uses a summary conclusion. It could have used any of the standard conclusions, but a prediction of what will happen if marijuana is legalized, or a call to action in the form of writing to lawmakers would also have been very effective. You may also want to point out that the essay is very near a minimum length for the summary type of conclusion.

Act

Write an essay . . . the required length.

Allow class time for this assignment so that students can have the advantage of developing ideas with the help of other students, and you can observe the process of their developing those ideas and writing the essay.

Students should choose a new topic for this assignment rather than one of the topics they have been practicing on.

Chapters 3 and 4 will make specific recommendations for revision, and students will be more capable of intelligent, complete revision at that time. For now, you may want to restrict your evaluation to such elements as use of the thesis sentence, topic sentences, paragraph development, introduction, and conclusion.

Chapter 3
Improvement Is the New Goal

Instructional Objectives

As a result of having studied this chapter, students will

1. learn three types of words that usually should be eliminated from their writing: foreign words, slang, and clichés

2. learn to look for awkward-sounding words and phrases, check for clarity of meaning, and proofread for spelling

3. learn to recognize and eliminate unnecessary information

4. learn to avoid wordiness by eliminating meaningless words and phrases

5. learn to avoid flowery language

6. learn to use transitional words and phrases precisely.

Vocabulary

Put the vocabulary words on the chalkboard and, if possible, leave them there for the duration of this chapter.

malign	correlate	affront	consolidate
rudimentary	resilience	stipend	laconic
implicit	enigma	scrupulous	condiment
macbre	incredulous	nefarious	savant
ignominy	hiatus	machiavellian	sentient

Motivation

Either by duplicating, using an overhead projector, or reading aloud, share the following quotations with your students. Each is from an official notice mailed to homeowners describing how property taxes will be determined and collected.

"When the name of the owner of any real estate is unknown, it shall be assessed without connecting therewith any name, but inscribing at the head of the page the words 'owners unknown', and such property, whether lands or town lots, shall be listed as nearly as practicable in the order of the numbers thereof."

"Any person who knowingly makes a false statement in making any verified statement or return, or in taking the oath required by sections 441.20 and 441.26, shall be guilty of perjury."

"If you are not satisfied that the foregoing assessment is correct, you may file a protest against such assessment with the Board of Review on or after April sixteenth, to and including May fifth, of the year of the assessment, such protest to be confined to the grounds specified in Section 441.37, Code of Iowa."

Ask students to suggest several ways the directions could be made clearer and more pleasant to read. While they may disagree among themselves about what should be done or the degree to which changes should be made, you can make the point that there is plenty of room for serious revision. Tell students that they are going to be studying some specific steps they can take to improve any piece of writing, including their own.

Some Don'ts and Some Do's

Discuss

1. Name and explain . . . example of each.
   Three types of words that should be avoided are:
   a. Foreign words used in place of common English equivalents. Discuss the difference between using foreign words to impress the reader and using foreign words that have become common in English usage. *Non sequitur* is a good example of a Latin term that is commonly used when the speaker refers to a statement that does not follow logically from what has been said previously. There is no precise English equivalent and, consequently, the term is considered acceptable. If students need a rule to guide them, tell them it is better to err on the side of simplicity.
   b. Slang in almost every situation. This is a good time to introduce the topics of establishing mood, creating a persona, and writing for a particular purpose and audience. Students will see that, while slang can be used effectively for specific purposes, thoughtless and purposeless use should be avoided.
   c. Clichés under almost any circumstances. Mention that some writers may occasionally be able to take a cliché and bring it to life with an original twist— "sadder but sillier," "the plot thins," and "the tried and still untrue."

2. What are three . . . improve your essay?
   Three specific steps can improve most student writing.
   a. Read the paper aloud with the purpose of spotting awkward-sounding words or phrases.
   b. Ask someone else to read the essay to see if the meaning is clear to a person who is not already familiar with it.
   c. Check spelling methodically. Viewing each line in reverse, right to left, allows the reader to concentrate on spelling alone and avoid being distracted by the content of each line.

Act

Students will probably find it easiest to point out foreign words, slang, and clichés. A few students may have such limited reading backgrounds that obvious clichés seem new to them. Praise for recognizing clichés will do more good than arguing that students should know a chiché when they see it. The real danger, remember, is that students will continue to thoughtlessly use the clichés that they hear every day. They'll have no problem with clichés they've never heard of.

1. Read the following . . . discussion questions above.

Suggest that the first paragraph may best be completely rewritten. The second paragraph could also be rewritten, but students should at least delete "for all intents and purposes" and "Faux pas."

2. Read the following . . . communicate more clearly?

Students should be able to spot misspellings and the many instances of unclear meaning. They will make a variety of suggestions for improvement. Ask students to read their improved versions, and note that there are many ways a paragraph's meaning can be made clearer.

Eliminate Unnecessary Information

Discuss

1. Explain the significance . . . as in architecture."

Although it may sound contradictory, "less is more" means that eliminating certain kinds of information has the overall effect of making an essay better than it was originally. Irrelevant or loosely related anecdotes and examples are not harmless diversions. They distract a reader from the purpose of the essay and actually have a negative effect on the writer's purpose.

2. Why do writers . . . unnecessary information? Explain.

Writers often include unnecessary information because they are not careful enough in deciding which facts to select and which to drop from their original ideas. Putting ideas on paper as they come to mind works well in the early stages of writing, but only the best and most relevant should survive the revision process.

Act

Rewrite the following . . . sentence is true.

Students will need to eliminate the last three sentences of each paragraph and replace them with information that supports the topic sentences.

For Your Journal

Donald Hall's comment . . . you have observed.

Tell students to make this a kind of private brainstorming session, each working independently. Encourage them to explain each of their examples as fully as possible.

In our society the concept of less being more might be difficult for some students. If they have trouble getting started, spend a few minutes considering the meanings of words like *gaudy, flashy,* and *ostentatious.*

Eliminate Unnecessary Words

Discuss

1. Name two causes . . . in student writing.
   a. Sometimes writers get so desperate for words that they are too easily pleased with their first efforts. The wordiness is overlooked in later drafts because everyone hates to throw out his or her hard work.
   b. Some writers take the guideline "write the way you talk" too literally, including all the empty words and phrases.
2. Writers of business . . . developed into clichés?
   Most of the wordy phrases with which students will be familiar are impressive sounding, if nothing else. The combination of sounding like a thoughtful person while using little or no thought make such phrases irresistible to many people. Some students will find it very difficult to accept simplicity as preferable to the wordy phrases they associate with business or school writing. In many cases their attitude has been encouraged by teachers who rewarded flowery writing. Be patient with them, but don't give in.

Act

Rewrite the following . . . directly and economically.

1. Twenty-five years ago computers were unheard of.
2. School consolidation will also combine athletic teams.
3. The first baseman hit a home run over the fence.
4. Refer to the original directions.
5. The tank struggled through the wet sand.
6. Always return library books.
7. Jim's winter coat is too large.
8. Shelly repeated what she said.
9. His convertible is green.
10. This is an anonymous poem.
11. I passed the test recently.
12. Her fiance is a little shorter than she.
13. The candidates have revised their positions repeatedly.
14. This plan is unique.
15. Jim tried to start the car.

Students will have many correct versions of these sentences. Some may want to argue about whether a given word is absolutely necessary. For instance, sentence 2 could also read "Consolidation will also combine athletic teams," assuming that readers would know from the context that school consolidation was the topic under discussion. Or sentence 3 could read "The first baseman hit a home run," assuming that all home runs go over the fence. While both assumptions are debatable, don't get caught in the trap of discussing it to the point where the purpose of the exercise is lost. Accept the answer, with reservations, and go on.

Keep It Simple

Discuss

1. Why would a . . . language when writing?
Most elegant writing results from the writer's belief that it makes him or her look intelligent. Students will usually recognize the fact that they also risk looking silly when they use words that are inappropriate for the situation or when they are not familiar with the connotations a word may carry.

2. Some elegant-sounding language . . . more complex term?
This is a good opportunity to remind students of their major purpose in writing—to communicate their thoughts to other people. Most readers today find it easier to understand the writer's message and are more comfortable with simpler language. The fact that simpler words usually communicate more effectively is reason enough to avoid the elegant-sounding terms.

Act

Rewrite these sentences . . . clear, simple language.
Students may disagree on the meanings of the original sentences and, therefore, have a variety of answers. Remind them that the very difficulty of translating the flowery language illustrates how easy it is to misunderstand the writer's message. Accept reasonable answers, while concentrating on the purpose of the activity—writing clearly and to the point.

1. Hand-eye coordination is an inherited trait.

2. Writers here should concentrate on the facts.

3. Your contract doesn't require a lawyer.

For Your Journal

Student writers sometimes . . . journal entry sounds.
Students will enjoy this journal entry, especially if you allow them to help each other with synonyms. When they have finished the paragraph that describes how their non-repetitious journal entry sounds, ask for volunteers to read their entries, and ask several students to come up with words to describe their synonyms.

Using Transitions

Discuss

1. Paragraphs are supposed . . . to other paragraphs?

Paragraphs are self-sufficient in the sense that they have their own beginning, middle, and end, and they form a complete support for topic sentences. But each paragraph is only one part of a much larger whole—the entire essay. Each paragraph is one element in the writer's explanation of his or her thesis sentence. Transitions link those reasons and help make the relationships between them clear. Well-thought-out transitions show how each paragraph fits into the whole and make clear to the reader why the writer put the information in that order.

2. Your essay should be . . . ideas in the essay?

If transitions are used carefully and correctly, they will show the relationship of each paragraph to the thesis, and they will show how each sentence is important to each paragraph.

Act

For each of the . . . the transitional words.

Accept any answers that use the transitional words appropriately. If some students use transitions carelessly, as if the transitions were identical in meaning, insist that they go back and, using the text as a guide, find an appropriate transition for the situation.

Chapter 4
Finding Your Writing Voice

Instructional Objectives

As a result of having studied this chapter, students will

1. practice writing in a way that reflects their own uniqueness

2. learn the difference between active voice and passive voice

3. normally write in active voice

4. learn to vary sentence length and type

5. direct their writing toward a specific audience

6. learn an acceptable format for completed essays.

Vocabulary

Put the vocabulary words on the chalkboard and, if possible, leave them there for the duration of this chapter.

inveigh	bereft	paradox	extraneous
insidious	noxious	solace	insipid
atrocious	berate	ostensible	cardinal
illicit	abscond	lithe	zenith
protagonist	epitome	eulogize	rasping

Motivation

Invite a writer from the community to speak to your class about the process and business of writing. This guest need not have written a best-seller; students will listen seriously and take the advice of someone who writes and publishes regularly. Brief the visitor about what the students are doing in class, and help students prepare questions ahead of time. They can ask about the visitor's writing habits, for example, or about a professional's point of view on revision.

As an alternative, have students bring to class examples of mail they or their parents have received asking for contributions or trying to sell something. As a class activity, examine how effectively the writing does its job. Ask "What is the purpose of this piece of mail?" "Is this plea for help effective?" "Do you think this letter will create much new business?" "Exactly what about the way this is written makes it effective?"

Be Yourself, Only Better

Discuss

1. What influences contribute . . . as a writer?

Family, hometown, friends, education, reading experiences, hobbies, memories, and religious background all contribute to an individual's uniqueness as a writer.

2. Why is it . . . and secure manner?

Students do not feel as comfortable writing as they do speaking, and sometimes the result is self-consciousness followed by artificiality.

Discuss with students the possibility that a lack of confidence can cause people to feel uncomfortable being themselves. Most students have experienced a situation in which they felt uncomfortable meeting new people and ended up giving the erroneous impression that they were cold or unfriendly. Explain that the same thing happens in the process of writing for an unfamiliar situation. The solution is not to avoid the situation but to be aware of the problem and remember to act relaxed and confident enough to be themselves.

Act

Write two paragraphs . . . suggest further revisions.

This activity is intended as practice in writing simply and directly. All evaluation of these paragraphs should be positive. You might want to have students attach to their papers a form that asks

1. What do you like about my paragraphs?

2. Can you suggest a simpler way to word one of my sentences?

Use Active Verbs

Discuss

1. What is active . . . example of each.

Active voice makes the subject of the sentence *perform* the action of the verb. The subject is active. It is doing something.

Kelli passed her driving test.

In passive voice, the subject of the sentence *receives* the action of the verb. The subject is passive. It is not doing anything.

The *driving test was passed* by Kelli.

2. Name two situations . . . improve your writing.

Remind students that most writers do not need to look for situations in which they can use passive constructions; accidental use is more than sufficient.

Passive voice is acceptable

a. when you want to focus attention on the action rather than the actor.

    b. when you do not know who performed the action and, therefore, cannot say a name.

    c. occasionally, for variety.

3. Why should the . . . usually be avoided?

Most of the results of passive verbs are negative. Passive voice sentences are often long and awkward; sometimes give a false sense of dignity; make it possible to deliberately withhold information; and produce indirect, often dull writing.

Act

1. Rewrite the following . . . direct active voice.

    a. I'll always remember the day dad took us to the circus.

    b. You can make an appointment for the first Monday of next month.

    c. John Riley explained the new seat belt law.

    d. The building inspector made three visits.

2. The following sentences . . . Explain your decisions.

Review the reasons given for using or avoiding the passive voice. Each of the sentences *can* be written with an active voice verb. Unless there is a specific purpose for using the passive, encourage students to try to make the sentences active. Be sure students understand that having a specific, logical reason is as important as the form they choose for each sentence.

For Your Journal

Americans are very . . . Use your imagination.

Students can give their sense of humor some freedom here. Creativity and imagination are more important than realism. Allow volunteers to share their ideas after everyone has finished.

Use Short, Varied Sentences

Discuss

Use both of these questions to emphasize the fact that achieving variety is more important than the length of any one sentence. Short sentences can be good. Long sentences can be good. A variety of sentence lengths and types is superior to either.

1. Why should you . . . of long sentences?

There is nothing wrong with long sentences. Often, they are necessary to communicate an idea, but a series of long sentences, with no variety, can become confusing and tiresome. Besides putting readers to sleep, they make ideas seem more difficult and complicated than they are.

2. Short sentences can also be a problem. Why?

In the same way that long sentences are not wrong in themselves, there is nothing bad about short sentences. A problem arises when long strings of them begin to sound childish or even sing-songy.

Act

1. Rewrite each of . . . variety of structures.

You may want to combine this exercise with a review of the different sentence types. A short discussion of simple, compound, complex, and compound-complex sentences will give students specific ideas about how to rewrite these sentences. Remind students to continue practicing what they have studied about simplifying language.

2. Rewrite this paragraph . . . more interesting ones.

Have several students read their completed revisions. Be sure they understand that the original does not contain any "wrong" sentences. The improvement will come from creating variety by breaking up a few of the tiresomely long constructions. Although some students' revisions will be more effective than others', their choice of which sentences to change is not as important as the change itself.

3. Rewrite the following . . . the choppy effect.

As with the previous paragraph, the choice of which sentences to change is not as important as the variety students create. Emphasize that the paragraph will be most effective if some of the sentences are left unchanged.

For Your Journal

People are always . . . as you write them.

Students should have fun with this journal entry. If you have students who could afford to relax a little, use this activity to make them less self-conscious. Again, some students will enjoy sharing their ideas with the class but, if some prefer to keep their journal private, respect that.

Remember Your Readers

Discuss

1. Why is it . . . picture your audience?

It is important to picture your audience because every audience is going to call for a slightly different emphasis in your writing. Everyone has a unique point of view, interests, and priorities. Once you have pictured the audience, you can picture yourself talking to that person. Then, you'll be better able to select information and the best wording possible.

If students have trouble understanding how they could write differently depending on the audience, point out how they adjust their manner of speaking every day depending on who they are speaking to. They don't speak to the principal of the school the same way they speak to their parents, and they don't speak to their friends the same way they speak to their brothers or sisters. Point out that this is not being two-faced; it is making reasonable adjustments to the situation. Ask for examples of other situations where they adjust their vocabulary, tone, and even sentence structure for the people around them.

2. Describe two methods . . . with your reader.
   Two methods that can improve communication with the reader are:

   a. Carry on an imaginary conversation with the audience. Figure out what arguments and wording would work best with this audience.

   b. Role-play the audience. Pretend that you are the other person. How would you feel about the topic if you were that person? How would you feel about this paper if you were the reader instead of the writer?

Act

List three assumptions . . . of these situations.

Make a master list of all the ideas students bring to class. Encourage students to see that three assumptions is minimal, and the more they can know about the audience, the easier it will be to know how to approach the writing task.

Also, point out that many bits and pieces of information may not be obvious but would be easy to learn. By the time the student is ready to write, he or she should have a fairly clear picture of the intended audience. For example, if students were to write a paper for topic 1 "writing to the mayor of your city about a proposed change in the zoning laws," a writer could find the following useful information without too much trouble: home address, present attitude toward zoning changes, reputation for openness to new ideas, attitudes toward business development, relationship with the city council, and reputation for concern about citizen's interests.

Checklist for Writers

Require students to follow the guidelines for handing in the final copy of their work. They will benefit from treating their work as something worthy of a neat, formal appearance. If you intend to adjust the directions in any way, do it now.

Chapter 5
Cause and Effect

Instructional Objectives

As a result of having studied this chapter, students will

1. recognize cause-and-effect reasoning as a thought pattern and as a method of organizing their writing

2. learn four steps involved in organizing a cause-and-effect essay

3. learn three pitfalls to avoid in cause-and-effect reasoning

4. learn to write two specialized types of introductions associated with cause-and-effect essays

5. review transitions that guide a reader's pattern of reasoning from cause to effect or effect to cause

6. read and evaluate a cause-and-effect essay

7. write a cause-and-effect essay.

Vocabulary

Put the vocabulary words on the chalkboard and, if possible, leave them there for the duration of this chapter.

redundant	consensus	execrate	caustic
disgruntled	mutable	conclave	superfluous
platitude	rampant	impediment	inanimate
ascertain	extraneous	antithesis	malediction
querulous	cartel	intrepid	banal

Motivation

On the day before beginning Chapter 5, divide the class into teams and give each team a list of cause-and-effect questions, such as those below. Students are to find and bring to class both the answer and the source of that answer. Offer points for each correct answer, and perhaps a small prize for the team scoring the most points.

1. Why do we give children the father's surname?

2. Why is English written from left to right?

3. Why is Hebrew written from right to left?

4. Why is Chinese written from the top to the bottom of the page?

5. Why do people eat three meals a day?

6. Why do men's suits have buttons on the sleeves?

7. Why were duels always held at dawn?

8. Why are cows milked from the right side?

9. Why are barber poles red and white?

10. Why are prisoners executed at dawn?

11. Why do people think opening an umbrella indoors is unlucky?

12. Why is election day on the Tuesday after the first Monday in November?

13. Why is north at the top of all maps?

The questions are intriguing enough to illustrate the fact that human beings have a natural curiosity about causes and effects. It's a small step from these relatively inconsequential questions to the reasons why people search for causes and effects of more important matters.

A Real-Life Application

Discuss

1. Why is cause-and-effect . . . in human experience?

It is part of human nature to want to understand why things happen. Since earliest times, people have been trying to pinpoint causes and predict effects so they can have some control over the world around them. By identifying causes or probable effects, we can try to prevent a recurrence of harmful events and make positive events happen again.

2. What practical purposes . . . from some action?

If we know why events occur, sometimes we can make those events happen again, prevent them from happening again, or control the degree to which they happen. In many instances, developing that ability is a matter of life or death.

If the Federal Aviation Administration determines that an airplane crash took place because of an engine failure, inspectors will check the engines on all similar planes in hopes of preventing another accident.

If we read that eating certain foods makes us more likely to have a heart attack or stroke, we can avoid those foods when possible.

Act

1. Write one paragraph . . . find a cause.

If students have trouble remembering examples of news events, suggest that they describe a specific *accident* that led people to look for causes. They could also recall discussions they may have had about an athletic team's success or failure. Sports discussions often consist of analyzing why one team is having problems or is being exceptionally successful.

2. Write a second paragraph . . . some likely possibilities?

Be sure students do not confuse cause with effect. If a paragraph describes a situation involving a string of causes and effects, be sure the writer makes clear the relationships involved. This is also a good time to begin pointing out that events are seldom motivated by a *single* cause.

3. Write one paragraph . . . can be expected.

If students have trouble remembering a suitable example, suggest that they describe a specific political contest or an advertisement they have seen. Typically, candidates or advertisers try to convince us that the future will be more pleasant if they get our vote or our money.

4. Write a second . . . those people expect.

Again, remind students that almost never does an event have only one effect. Also, when a paragraph involves interrelated causes and effects, be certain that students can make the distinction clear.

For Your Journal

In the first half . . . the schools, the country?

Students are likely to feel knowledgeable about the topic of divorce, either from their own family situations or from those of friends. Expect that their opinions will be colored by personal experiences and that they might have wide-ranging and insightful opinions. Remind students to treat the whole topic, all the way from causes to effects.

Four Guides to Basic Organization

Discuss

1. In what way . . . effects be dangerous?

Oversimplifying causes or effects can easily lead to overlooking additional significant ideas. The person who blames his or her inability to get a job on some unfortunate physical characteristic—shortness, tallness, overweight, underweight—might possibly have a point but, at the same time, be overlooking other, more important causes: lack of education, grooming, or interview skills.

2. What process can . . . to avoid oversimplification?

It is a good idea to begin by barainstorming as many ideas as possible. Make a list of all the causes or effects that come to mind, reserving judgment about which might be most significant.

3. One of the steps . . . expect to find?

Cause-and-effect relationships commonly involve long chains of events with many intermediate steps. In the example about high divorce rates causing juvenile crime, not one of the steps can be ignored or treated lightly. Each one is important, and if any link in the chain proves to be false, the whole connection between divorce and juvenile crime is at least seriously weakened.

4. Why should you . . . planning your presentation?

You must distinguish between degrees of importance because you probably haven't space to treat all your causes and effects equally. You must make decisions about which ones will be emphasized.

Also, most readers have enough sense to realize that not all causes or effects are of equal value. If you give too little space to major factors, or too much space to unimportant ones, you seem to have a faulty view of the situation, and your argument will be weakened.

Finally, degrees of importance could determine the order in which you want to present causes or effects.

Act

1. Consider the following as effects . . . causes of each.

Have students work in small groups to brainstorm significant causes. Encourage the groups to make lists of ten causes and narrow that list to what they believe are the six most significant.

2. Consider the following as causes . . . effects of each.

Again, have students work in groups to list the most meaningful effects possible.

3. Choose one of . . . than the others.

This is a good time to begin requiring that students be able to defend their opinions with factual evidence. Insist that they think through their ranking carefully. Do not accept "because" or "I just think so" as explanations.

Three Traps to Avoid

Discuss

1. How can time . . . search for causes?

People like to think of the world as an orderly place, and our eagerness to link events as cause and effect often leads us to imagine relationships that do not exist. When we are looking for causes behind an event, time order can provide clues, but time order can also be misleading if the relationship is coincidental. Events that take place at the same time or one immediately following the other are not necessarily related. In addition to the time relationship, a true causal relationship must exist.

2. Explain the difference . . . of your own.

Events do not occur in isolation. If two events occur almost simultaneously, it is possible that one caused the other, but it is just as likely that both are simultaneous results of some earlier event.

For instance, if a student can't study because she has a terrible headache, she may treat the headache with aspirin. If that takes care of the problem, she may not have any concern. If the headache comes back the next day, however, she should consider the possibility that the headache is not a cause of her problem but a symptom of some greater problem. Perhaps she is suffering from eyestrain and needs reading glasses. As long as she continues to treat the symptom—the headache—instead of the problem—eyestrain—her troubles will continue.

3. What is the advantage . . . in your explanation?

The essay will be more persuasive if you can keep your reader from being distracted by misleading causes or effects. If you do not mention a cause or effect because you realize it is unimportant, you cannot be certain that your reader will feel the same way. You may need to point out the fact that this cause or that effect appears to be of consequence but really isn't, and then explain why.

Finally, if you don't mention the false cause or effect, you may appear to be overlooking something important, and you will lose credibility.

Act

Look at each . . . explain your choices.

1. a. probable cause
    b. symptom
    c. probable cause
    d. symptom; possible contributor
    e. symptom

2. a. symptom
    b. symptom
    c. symptom; possible contributor
    d. symptom
    e. symptom

More important than the label given each of these possible causes is the explanation that should follow. In a few cases, students may see a symptom as encouraging or contributing to the effect. For instance, under "Our football team had a poor season," they may point out that although the fan support probably grew worse with each game as a result of the team's poor season, the players could well have played worse as a result of the loss of support. Encourage such answers because they show the student is examining all possible causes carefully rather than accepting the situation at face value.

For Your Journal

People approach unpleasant . . . into the future.

Remind students that they have been discussing how to accurately identify causes and effects. This is an opportunity to thoroughly think through what could become a long chain of events.

The Parts and the Whole

Discuss

1. What is the thesis of Clint's essay?
    The thesis is "Ocean dumping must be outlawed."

2. List the subpoints that support the thesis.

Subpoints supporting the thesis are:

a. Although small amounts of waste will probably do little harm, large amounts destroy ocean life by spreading diseases and depleting the water of its oxygen supply.

b. A secondary result is that ocean dumping is posing a serious threat to the seafood industry.

c. Finally, garbage dumping pollutes coastal waters and beaches, affecting vacationers, home owners, and resort operators.

3. What is the . . . in the essay?

In an effort to convince his readers that garbage must not be disposed of in the ocean, Clint is showing all the horrifying effects of ocean dumping.

4. Look at his . . . it be improved?

Students should be able to provide at least one way in which the point is handled well and one suggestion for improvement. For instance, the first subpoint has a strong topic sentence and many effective examples of disease caused by garbage in the ocean. Clint shows the relationships between examples, and he explains the significance of his examples when that is necessary.

On the negative side, some of the examples in Clint's first body paragraph are not actually disease related and, consequently, the topic sentence is not 100 percent accurate. The topic sentence could be broadened slightly to include all the examples given.

5. Clint devotes three . . . The disadvantages?

Clint probably divided his first subpoint into three paragraphs because one long paragraph would have been visually unattractive and possibly tiring for the reader. It would have filled one entire typed page, or two to three handwritten pages.

The greatest advantages to breaking up such a long paragraph are that it is easier to read and is visually less threatening to a reader.

The disadvantage comes from the fact that, since the paragraph is supposed to be written entirely in support of the one topic sentence, there are no natural places to break the paragraph. For instance, the final examples, involving sea turtles and sea lions being harmed by plastic debris, would seem more natural if they were not separated from the statement about 2,000,000 sea birds and 100,000 marine animals dying as a result of plastic being dumped into the ocean.

Act

Your school's homecoming . . . during this period.

Remind students to apply the fundamental principles of persuasive writing to their essays. Brainstorm, select, drop, and cluster ideas. Use a thesis sentence, support that thesis with clear explanations and examples, and write an effective introduction and conclusion.

Chapter 6
Definition

Instructional Objectives

As a result of having studied this chapter, students will

1. be able to define the term *abstract language*

2. be able to define the term *concrete language*

3. become familiar with levels of abstraction

4. learn the difference between a dictionary definition and an extended definition

5. learn five methods of developing an extended definition: naming characteristics, giving examples, explaining purpose, comparing and contrasting, and giving analogies

6. read and evaluate a definition essay

7. write a definition essay.

Vocabulary

Put the vocabulary words on the chalkboard and, if possible, leave them there for the duration of this chapter.

dilettante	voracious	pedantic	hypothesis
bellicose	imminent	reticent	vernacular
gamut	recompense	peruse	adulation
compendium	esoteric	labyrinth	resilient
adversity	intrepid	infallible	reprisal

Motivation

Ask each student to take out a half-sheet of notebook paper. Explain that you want each of them to write two definitions, one on each side of the paper. There is to be no talking or sharing of ideas, and each definition should be at least a full sentence.

For the first word, have students define *love, patriotism, intellectual*, or some equally abstract term. For the second word, have students define *book, pencil, purse*, or an equally concrete term. Then ask students to read their answers.

They will, of course, have a more difficult time defining the abstract terms, and they will probably produce a greater variety of definitions. The concrete terms are likely to be easier and much more similar. Lead a short discussion on why the first definition was so difficult compared to the second.

The students' first reaction is likely to be, "That's simple. The first word is more complicated and the second was an easy thing." Don't settle for that. Students should at least begin to think about the fact that some words stand for real things that can be detected by the senses. They are relatively easy to define. Other words are non-image-producing and refer to concepts we can know only through our minds. Those can be very difficult to define. Then assign the reading.

Abstract and Concrete Language

Discuss

1. How can abstract . . . of your own.

Abstract words can cause a second level of disagreement when people fail to clarify terms that can have more than one interpretation. Abstractions almost always mean different things to different people. For example, if a writer uses a word like *patriotism* without explaining what the word means to him or her, the writer and the reader can be thinking of entirely different ideas. To one person patriotism might mean flying the flag. To another, it might mean supporting an unpopular person's right to freedom of speech.

2. How can abstract . . . of your own.

If abstract words are used carelessly and without clarification, they can create the illusion that a subject is simple when it is not. If a person is called a "good student," that label may be accepted without question by many people. But other people might argue if they realized that their definition of a good student and the speaker's definition were not even similar. What grades does a good student get? How many times can you get a *B* and still be a good student? How hard does the student have to work? Does getting good grades in easy courses count? Can you get a *C* in a very difficult course and still be a good student? The question of what makes a good student is not an easy one.

Act

1. Reread the story . . . are also abstract.

The story is, of course, filled with abstractions. Point out: successful season, football types, take us seriously, boring, school spirit, athletic ability, violence, brawny type, hard work, and good physical condition.

2. Pick three of . . . could be interpreted.

Students should see that the abstract terms are always ambiguous and can be interpreted in many ways. A *successful season* could require improvement from the previous season, a record of more wins than losses, a conference championship, or a state championship. The definition can change depending on the standards of the speaker.

For Your Journal

In *Gulliver's Travels* . . . take a humorous approach.

If your students are familiar with George Orwell's *1984*, you might get them started by discussing some of the questions raised about language in that book. The Party was simplifying language, doing away with words so that in the future people would have no means of expressing treasonous thoughts, most of which were abstractions like *freedom* and *liberty*. If the word for an idea no longer exists, can people talk about it? Perhaps more important, can they think about it?

Scale of Abstraction

Discuss

1. Why is it . . . or exclusively concrete?

Words do not easily fit into such neat little categories. While some are extremely abstract or extremely concrete, most fall somewhere in the middle and are abstract or concrete only in relation to other terms that could be used.

2. Why is the . . . a set of words?

Whether a word is abstract or concrete is all a matter of degree. While people refer to words as being one or the other, there are many degrees of abstraction or concreteness.

Act

Name four abstract . . . is more abstract.

Students may need help in getting started.

a. furniture, table, picnic table

b. animal, pet, dog

c. communicate, discuss, quarrel

d. utensil, silverware, butter knife

Types of Definition

Discuss

1. Under what circumstances would . . . be complete enough.

The dictionary definition is usually adequate when defining a relatively concrete term or an abstraction that is not particularly complicated. A word such as *ombudsman* can probably be defined clearly in a sentence or two. Once you have explained that the word refers to an official appointed by an organization to investigate complaints against people in authority, there is not a lot of room for misunderstanding. However, if the word is extremely important to your purpose in writing, it may call for elaboration.

2. Under what circumstances . . . definition is necessary.

An extended definition may become necessary any time a word is abstract or controversial. If it is important that the reader agree with the writer's interpretation of a word, or at least understand the writer's interpretation, an extended definition becomes very useful. If a committee is trying to choose your school's Outstanding Student of the Year, not having agreed first on what *outstanding* means could cause a lot of unnecessary argument.

Act

Without using a . . . in the class.

Remind students to review the text's explanation and illustrations of dictionary definitions. You may also find it useful to have them write the definitions in two columns, one for the general class and one for the differentiation.

term	classification	differentiation
house	building	used as a living quarters
window	opening	for admitting light or air
brick	building material	of clay hardened by heat
senator	member	of the upper house of the United States Congress
chair	furniture	with four legs and a back, used to support a person
table	furniture	with flat slab supported on four legs

For Your Journal

You and your . . . to call someone?

Ask students to share their ideas. This is a good time to talk about the connotations associated with words and the dangers of assuming that "everybody knows" what a term means.

Methods of Extended Definition

Discuss

1. When naming characteristics . . . you are defining?

You must use only those characteristics that make your word stand out from others like it. If your definition of a word could apply to two or more other words, there is always the chance that your reader will not know which meaning you have in mind.

2. Name three abstract . . . important in each?

If students have difficulty getted started, suggest the following possibilities: a *vacation,* a *good pet,* and *nursing care* are all abstractions and all can be described in terms of what they are supposed to accomplish.

3. A comparison can . . . begin to overlap? Why?

The fact that the methods might seem to overlap is of no importance. The purpose of an extended definition is to explain the idea to the reader, and being able to label the method used doesn't contribute to that purpose.

Act

For each term . . . at least once.

Each of the terms could be defined with several methods. The purpose of the activity is not to decide which method would produce the best definition but to practice applying the methods to a number of situations.

Writing a Definition Essay

Discuss

1. What is the thesis . . . is it stated?

   The thesis is "Anyone who is incapable of living a happy and fulfilled life in our society is truly needy." Students may debate how well the thesis is stated, but it does reflect the writer's idea that being "happy" and "fulfilled" are crucial. Those terms, of course, need to be clarified in the essay.

2. List the supporting . . . intend to develop?

   Supporting points are:

   a. The most obviously needy people are the homeless.

   b. Anyone who does not have a good education is usually doomed to a life of hard physical work, little pay, and little time for pleasure.

   c. Another thing that can cause misery is continuing poor health.

   d. Furthermore, everyone has needs beyond the physical, and to deny these needs is cruel and inhumane.

3. Analyze any two . . . should take place.

   Students should be able to cite strengths and weaknesses. Ask about topic sentences, explanations, and examples. Insist on specific comments rather than generalities. "Look at the fifth paragraph. I like the way he combined the topic sentence with a transition to show that he was going into an entirely new kind of neediness" is better than "I guess most of it was pretty clear," or "He had lots of explanation."

4. How concrete is . . . truly needy people?

   He gives many examples of the people he means. When he talks about the homeless, for instance, he tells what they need—food, clothing, shelter—and how they get by from day to day—begging, prostitution, robbery, and eating out of garbage cans. When he talks about people with poor health, he describes them as having extreme cases of arthritis or hard-to-cure illnesses like cancer, and needing expensive medicines.

   He does not go so far as to "show" what he means by examples of specific cases or by naming people he is familiar with who fit the mold of "needy people."

5. How good is the introduction? Explain.

   The introduction brings up the topic in a natural-sounding manner, though it may be a little abrupt. Can students suggest other, at least equally good, ways of bringing up the topic of truly needy people?

6. How good is the conclusion? Explain.

Again, point out that the conclusion does its job well. But can students suggest other conclusions that might have worked equally well?

Act

Write a carefully . . . with that in mind.

Students can use any word that they find interesting and challenging. Abstract terms used in the story at the beginning of the chapter might be a good place to look for ideas.

Another possibility is to take a term suggested by a current event and ask students to develop and explain their own views. At a time when flag burning is in the news, ''respect for the flag'' might be an interesting topic. At a time when citizen protest is in the news, ''freedom of speech'' could work as well. If seat belt laws are the topic of the day, ''personal rights'' or ''responsibility'' might be good abstractions to define because students will have been thinking about the topics.

Chapter 7
The Classification Essay

Instructional Objectives

As a result of having studied this chapter, students will

1. be able to define *classification*

2. recognize classification as a universal method of organizing complex information

3. learn three uses of classification in their writing

4. learn four principles of effective classification

5. learn five guidelines for writing a classification essay

6. read and evaluate a classification essay

7. write a classification essay.

Vocabulary

Put the vocabulary words on the chalkboard and, if possible, leave them there for the duration of this chapter.

faction	dissension	proficiency	nebulous
abolish	archives	aggression	mercenary
discriminate	magnanimous	guise	deterrent
credulity	hypothetical	append	impromptu
prudent	ruthless	forbearance	placid

Motivation

Initiate a discussion of popular movies with the class by asking students to write down the names of the best one or two films they have seen this year. As they are thinking, draw five or six columns on the chalkboard without labeling the columns in any way. After the students have made their decisions, ask each to name his or her choices.

As students name their movies, write the titles on the chalkboard, grouping them with similar types. The columns should remain unlabeled, but you might think of them as comedy, horror, romance, western, science fiction, documentary, and any other categories suggested by the students' choices. By the time you have listed eight or ten films, the students will understand the system and be able to predict where a title is going to go even before you start to write. If they are at all slow catching on, ask "Let's see. *Back to the Future 4*. Where should that go?"

When all the titles are recorded, ask students to think of a label to write at the top of the column. They may not use the same category titles you would, but accept reasonable answers. Then ask, "What are the advantages of listing the films this way instead of in the order you named them?" Expect such answers as, "People who feel like a comedy can find one easily." "If you aren't familiar with a movie, at least you know a little of what it might be like." Or "If you hate documentaries, you can avoid any movie on that list." Point out that you could have broken the list into columns representing "4-star" movies, "3-star" movies, and so on. Or you could have arranged them by audience suitability—G, PG, PG-13, R or NC-17. Each method of dividing the list would have provided a specific kind of information to anyone reading the list.

Then assign the reading of Chapter 7.

The Mind Needs Order

Discuss

1. Why is classification . . . with everyday experiences?

The human mind needs a system. It can learn more and use knowledge to better advantage when knowledge is organized. People process so much information that they would be overwhelmed without some kind of organization.

2. How does classification . . . amounts of information?

When people break masses of information into logical parts, they begin to see relationships between pieces of the information. Those relationships make it possible to deal with the information systematically. If a person observes animals randomly, nature seems chaotic, but if a scientist organizes those animals into groups of invertebrates, fish, reptiles, amphibians, birds, and mammals, the animal kingdom becomes manageable.

Act

1. In as many . . . used by the teacher.

Keep the activity easy and don't be concerned if a student's systems of classification seem shallow. They will have opportunities to challenge themselves later. For now, be sure that everyone understands the concept.

2. Classify yourself in . . . different characteristics.

As with the last activity, don't be overly concerned if students are choosing safe, easy classifications for themselves. You might, however, encourage a few students to go beyond the most obvious answers by asking if they can break their answers down a little further. For instance, the student who describes herself as a "Democrat" might be asked how she sees herself as fitting into the Democratic party. "Do you think of yourself as a liberal Democrat or a conservative Democrat?" If most students describe themselves as being "middle class," point out that a huge majority of Americans describe themselves as middle class. "Where do you see yourself in relation to the rest of those people?"

For Your Journal

People are often . . . advantage over others?

This journal entry involves a more serious topic than earlier ones. Students are extremely concerned about how others see them, and many students will see themselves and others as being treated unjustly. When students have finished writing, and perhaps shared some of their thoughts, mention that this is a topic that could be developed into a full essay sometime in the future.

Classification in Your Writing

Discuss

1. Explain in three . . . classification in writing.

First, the writer makes a list of facts or ideas that seem to support his or her thesis. Those facts or ideas all come from one classification.

Second, the writer clusters those facts or ideas into natural groupings. Those are more classifications.

Third, the writer can use classification as the major interest and purpose of the essay.

2. Classification is probably . . . in an essay?

Sometimes the classifications themselves can become of such interest that they deserve to be discussed on their own merits. Instead of using classifications to develop and organize ideas, the writer tells about the classifications simply because they are so interesting. Showing why someone or something belongs in a particular classification becomes the purpose and the main interest of the essay.

Act

Choose four of . . . a topic of your own.

The activity is intended to get students thinking about some of the difficulties involved in classifying. The next section of the text will present some guidelines for developing classifications, and students will be more receptive to those guidelines if they have seen that classifying is more complicated than just applying descriptive terms to a topic. For instance, a student might categorize coaches as

a. good coaches
b. bad coaches
c. men coaches
d. women coaches

e. experienced coaches
f. inexperienced coaches
g. understanding coaches
h. football coaches

A short discussion will convince the student that an essay using these categories would be hopelessly confusing. Tell the class they will be studying some guidelines that will make classification much less confusing.

For Your Journal

Some people tend . . . as a result?

Initially, most students will not have thought of luck as falling into distinct classifications, but this may supply some ideas for another essay. You might also remind students of Chapter 6 and ask, "How might your definition of *luck* affect the way you answer this question?"

Preparing to Write

Discuss

Explain why a . . . least three classifications.

Most of the time, naming only two classifications is a sign that the writer is over-king something. Almost anything worth discussing is more involved than that and be divided further. Also, two classifications don't offer much to work with if the writer intends to base a whole essay on them.

2. Why is it . . . classification in an essay?

Trying to classify anything by more than one principle of classification creates an impossibly confusing situation. Ask the students for examples of mixing classifications inappropriately.

3. Point out the . . . in an outline.

Students will find many weaknesses, but you can suggest the following as logical answers:

a. Most often, an essay needs at least three classes.

b. Each of the groups conceivably could be used for an essay. The second, sex, wouldn't make a good basis for division, of course.

c. The classes listed are not natural divisions of any single classification system. They will result in a confusing essay.

d. The third class, Protestant, includes many major American religions and should be divided further.

e. The class "Parochial" does not belong in this list. It is not one of the natural divisions of this classification system.

Act

People or things . . . for later use.

This outline will be used later in the chapter. Remind students to limit their topic to something that they could write about in 500 to 600 words. The outline should have at least three classifications, and be confined to only one principle of classification.

Developing Your Essay

Discuss

1. Why is it . . . including an example.

If you purposely leave out a characteristic that some people might expect but that you think is inappropriate, many readers will think the characteristic is being overlooked. For instance, if you are classifying sports cars, one of the classifications might be called "classic sports cars." Many people would say that the "classic sports car" must be a convertible but, if you disagree, you should explain why you feel that way.

With another topic, you might want to include a characteristic that many people would leave out. If there is room for disagreement, you need to explain why you chose to include that characteristic. For instance, if you think the "classic sports car" must have a manual transmission, you should explain why because some sports cars have automatic transmissions, and their owners don't think of them as being in any way inferior.

2. Under what circumstances . . . Give an example.

With some topics, not all of the classifications are equally complex. In describing card games, you might have one class called "children's games." Since those tend to be relatively simple, you will probably use little space in explaining them, but you might need a lot more space to describe a group you called "sophisticated games."

Act

In the last . . . least two examples.

Review the four principles for developing the essay. For this assignment, students need to remember to explain themselves as thoroughly as necessary in one well-developed paragraph. Examples should be described in as much detail as possible.

A Whole Essay

Discuss

1. What is the thesis of Eric's essay?

Eric's thesis is "People's attitudes toward football show some interesting varieties of human nature."

2. What is the . . . used in this essay?

The single principle of classification is fans' attitudes about actually attending football games. The topic is football fans, and they could have been classified according to several other principles: experience playing football, knowledge of the game, sportsmanship, emotional involvement with their teams, or the importance of football compared to other aspects of their lives.

3. Eric could have . . . suppose he didn't?

Students will see many possibilities here. Explain that there is at least one very likely reason.

The purpose of Eric's essay seems to be as much entertainment as it is a serious examination of football fans. With three categories, he is able to humorously describe each, give several examples, and stop before the number of categories gets confusing. If he had used, for instance, five categories, the reader could easily have become confused. Worse yet, the subject might have become tiresome.

4. What do you . . . Why?

Eric's transitions are an imaginative method of reminding the reader of what has come before as well as announcing what comes next. He avoids the basic "first, second, and third" approach while still leading the reader through the different types of fans. Ask students to note how the last sentence of paragraph 2 begins the transition from "die-hard fan" to "fair-weather fan," and the first sentence of paragraph 3 completes that transition.

5. How has Eric . . . Explain.

Eric uses the thesis sentence to do more than simply announce that he is going to classify football fans by their attendance at games. He gives the paper more interest by including his own point of view—not only are there three different types of fans, but those fans reveal some interesting varieties of human nature. He then shows why the die-hard fan is to be admired, the fair-weather fan is to be looked down upon, and the couch-potato fan is merely laughable.

Act

Write an essay . . .700 word essay.

Remind students that they wrote two journal entries for this chapter that might make a good beginning for the classification essay. Also, this essay can be serious or silly, and the students will learn the principles of classification from either approach.

Assign an outline of the essay before actual writing begins. When students complete their thesis and topic sentence outlines, you can confer with each to be sure they are limiting the topic appropriately, using at least three classifications, using only one principle of classification, making classifications complete, and expressing an original point of view about the subject.

In your final evaluation for content, keep in mind the text's instructions about explaining the treatment of characteristics, developing the classifications thoroughly, and acknowledging complications.

Chapter 8
Comparison and Contrast

Instructional Objectives

As a result of having studied this chapter, students will

1. recognize comparison and contrast as common decision-making tools

2. learn when to use comparison, when to use contrast, and when to combine the advantages of each

3. be aware of the special attention needed when writing a comparison and contrast thesis

4. learn the two common structural patterns used in comparison and contrast essays

5. read and evaluate a comparison and contrast essay

6. write a comparison and contrast essay.

Vocabulary

Put the vocabulary words on the chalkboard and, if possible, leave them there for the duration of this chapter.

conducive	anarchy	redundant	enhance
attrition	peruse	latent	tortuous
qualm	adroit	equitable	infirm
ameliorate	propriety	acquiesce	predacious
oscillate	impasse	indiscretion	vacillate

Motivation

Tell students to imagine for a moment the following situation:

A local woman, Elizabeth Ohler, died last month and left $50,000 to the school district. Along with the $50,000 came directions to establish a trust fund that would allow the students to make two annual awards for teaching excellence, one for $3,000 and the other for $1,000. The awards will go to any two teachers in the school district, kindergarten through twelfth grade. Ms. Ohler said in her will that high school students were to have the responsibility of choosing the recipients because she thought it important that "students should carefully consider what makes a good teacher."

Tell students to think back over all the teachers they have had (not including this year) and pick the best two. Then, in their journals, tell which teacher should get the $3,000 and which the $1,000, and justify the decision with as many specific reasons as they can think of.

When students have finished, ask them to answer the following questions.

a. What makes a decision like this difficult?

b. Can you think of any ways the decision could be made easier?

Comparison or Contrast?

Discuss

1. In what kinds . . . a specific example.

A writer might want to emphasize similarities if his or her purpose were to make a person, a product, or an idea look good through association with something else that people admire. For instance, an inexpensive product will look most attractive if it compares favorably with an expensive product. A new idea will attract supporters if it compares favorably with an accepted idea.

2. When might concentrating . . . a specific example.

A writer might want to emphasize differences if his or her purpose were to make a person, a product, or an idea look good because it is superior to something else that is familiar to the audience. For instance, a new running shoe will look best if it has specific advantages over an older model shoe.

3. In some cases . . . a specific situation.

Purpose decides the best approach. If the purpose is not to take sides or show why one is better than the other but to create as complete and balanced a picture as possible, the writer will want to point out both similarities and differences. For instance, a family trying to decide whether to buy a two-door sedan or a mini-van would want to look at all the advantages and disadvantages of each. The best way to do that would be to list all the ways they are similar and all the ways they are different—make a complete comparison and contrast.

Act

For each of . . . Explain your answer.
1. The answer depends on circumstances. The salesperson may need to show how the ten-speed compares favorably with something more expensive, or how it contrasts with something less expensive. The correct approach depends on the salesperson's circumstances and purpose.
2. Use a combination to make an informed decision.
3. Use a combination to make an informed decision.
4. Use a combination. Similarities may be necessary to convince the reader that your argument has any merit, and contrast would allow you to show that one can actually be worse than the other.
5. Use contrast to show one is better than the other.
6. Use comparison to show all the similarities.

7. Use contrast to show the advantages of one or the other.

For Your Journal

People are not . . . are really like?

   Encourage students to have fun with this journal entry. They should, of course, see the obvious connection between the topic and the text's discussion of contrast. If some prefer to argue that the premise of the assignment is unfair and their favorite personalities are exactly what they seem to be, those students will benefit as much by developing a comparison. They can show how the person lives up to the image projected. Whichever side they take, remember that these are *their* journals, but praise those students who provide evidence for their opinions.

The Thesis Statement

Discuss

1. How is the . . . essay particularly challenging?

   The thesis statement of a comparison and contrast essay includes two factors. It tells the purpose of the essay, and it says that you are going to accomplish that purpose through the use of comparison, contrast, or a combination of the two. Some writers have a tendency to act as if the purpose of the essay is limited to showing similarities and differences, but the effective thesis statement will remind the reader that there is a greater purpose behind the comparison and contrast.

2. In what way . . . and contrast essay?

   It is possible to write a comparison and contrast essay that is strictly informative and doesn't take sides, but more often the ultimate purpose is to support an argument. Even when the essay does not support an argument, the writer usually has a unifying reason for showing all the similarities and differences.

Act

For five of . . . ideas, or people.

   All the topics can generate multiple answers. A correct thesis sentence will include the two parts of a comparison and contrast thesis: It will state the purpose of the essay and give a signal that the purpose will be supported through comparison and contrast. For example, "A careful look at the pitching of the Chicago Cubs and the St. Louis Cardinals clearly shows that the Cubs should have a better overall record."

Organization

Discuss

1. Why are having . . . and contrast essay?

   Because the writer discusses two different things, dividing the discussion between several similarities and differences, even the simplest comparison and contrast essay has more elements than most other essays. Using a simple structure and outlining the essay before beginning to write will lessen the chance of confusion as much as possible.

2. Why is the . . . for shorter essays?

The opposing pattern is most effective for shorter essays because it allows the reader to receive a separate total impression of each object, person, or idea being discussed. The entire first half of the essay deals with the first topic, the second half deals with the second topic. Since the opposing pattern does not switch back and forth between topics, there is less chance for confusion.

3. How does the . . . subjects being discussed?

The alternating pattern emphasizes the individual characteristics because its topic sentences deal with characteristics rather than the objects, persons, or ideas being compared and contrasted.

4. Why is the . . . pattern to use?

Most often, the opposing pattern works best for short essays, and the alternating pattern works best for long essays, but no rule governs their use. When the essay is neither particularly long nor particularly short, the writer can use the advantages of either structure.

The alternating pattern works well if an emphasis on individual characteristics is important, or if the topics being compared and contrasted have a large number of characteristics to be discussed.

The opposing pattern works well if the emphasis belongs with the things being compared and the number of characteristics is limited.

Act

In the previous . . . for each pattern.

Tell students to use the structure that seems most appropriate for the topic. Thesis sentences may need to be changed slightly to match the pattern used.

For Your Journal

In his book . . . may not have considered?

Students will probably not worry about whether their journal entry turns out to be mostly comparison, mostly contrast, or a mixture. In the same way, they may not concern themselves with the choice between alternating or opposing patterns. Allow them to write freely to get their ideas down on paper. You might want to point out, however, that if they turned this journal entry into an essay, they would reorganize it into the form that would communicate most effectively with the reader.

A Comparison and Contrast Essay

Discuss

1. What pattern, opposing . . . chose this pattern?

The essay is written in the opposing pattern. Brad probably chose this pattern for several reasons.

First, the essay contrasts two time periods—"then" and "now"—and Brad wanted to emphasize the time periods rather than any of the individual changes that he experienced. Second, the paper is reasonably short so the characteristics associated with "then" can still be remembered as the reader goes into the "now." Last, the very limited number of characteristics makes it unnecessary to use the alternating pattern.

2. What is Brad's . . . of his change?

Brad's thesis is actually in the form of two sentences. They could, of course, have been written as one compound sentence. "I once worked for superior grades, participated in classes, and maintained a first-rate attitude. But this year, my attitude has shifted gears." The thesis sentence suggests that the change has been a negative one, but Brad doesn't seem too worried about it.

3. Write a brief . . . of the essay?

I. Then
  A. Made good use of my time
  B. Dashed from class to class to avoid tardiness
  C. Homework was easy
  D. Always had homework assignments completed

II. Now
  A. Wastes class time
  B. Strolls into class at the last moment
  C. Homework is more difficult
  D. Always struggling to catch up with homework

Brad does treat the major characteristics of his behavior in both parts of the essay, but he words them in such a way that it is not overly obvious.

4. In what way . . . of his "burnout"?

The paper is persuasive in the sense that he blames his change on increased homework, decreased time to complete that homework, and frustration. At the same time, his word choice—"My work ethic has changed," "My once well managed day is in chaos," and "My fine-tuned machine needs a trip to the repair shop"—suggests that he knows further change is necessary and the change must come from him.

5. How did Brad . . . Why not?

The introduction and conclusion are tied together when Brad compares himself to a machine. In the introduction he writes, "My gauges read all systems go; now the red warning lights flicker constantly," and "This year, my attitude has shifted gears." In the conclusion he writes, "My fine-tuned machine needs a trip to the repair shop."

Students may not agree on the effectiveness of his comparison, but you might suggest that, at the very least, it seems appropriate and does tie the introduction and conclusion together.

Act

At the beginning . . . the following list.

For this assignment, students should use both comparison and contrast so that they can examine all aspects of the choice they are to make.

Thesis sentences may differ. If the writer makes a clear choice between two possibilities, the thesis should convey that message, but if the writer simply examines all the advantages and disadvantages without making a choice, the thesis will take a different form:

> "A comparison between the state university and Grinnell College clearly shows Grinnell to be the best choice for me."
>
> or
>
> "With my career goals, making the choice between a major in Marketing or Fashion Design seems almost impossible."

Leave the choice of opposing or alternating pattern to the student, but most essays will be short enough and have few enough characteristics to make the opposing pattern the best choice.

Chapter 9
The Inductive Argument

Instructional Objectives

As a result of having studied this chapter, students will

1. be able to define and understand the process of inductive reasoning

2. understand the necessity of induction despite the possibility of error

3. learn five guidelines for the use of inductive evidence

4. learn where and how to gather evidence that supports inductive reasoning

5. read and evaluate an essay that is based on inductive reasoning

6. write an essay that is based on inductive reasoning.

Vocabulary

Put the list of vocabulary words on the chalkboard and, if possible, leave them there for the duration of this chapter.

assiduous	expunge	equivocal	relegate
expurgate	lugubrious	germane	ingenuous
cumulative	expiate	semblance	negligent
neophyte	spurious	dearth	benign
assimilate	affable	blatant	vacillate

Motivation

On a blank sheet of paper, draw a grid made up of 25 squares, five horizontal and five vertical. Letter the columns and number the rows.

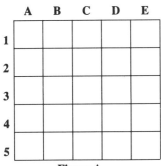

Figure A

On the grid, draw a simple figure. It could be a flower, a triangle, a pencil, or some more complicated figure.

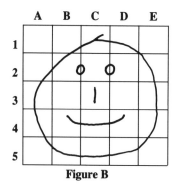

Figure B

Put a blank grid on the chalkboard or overhead projector and tell students they are going to play a game of skill. Each student will take a turn. The first student will pick one square—B-2, for instance—and you will show the class what part of the picture is on that square.

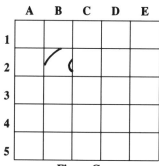

Figure C

Then the second student will select a square, and you will show what part of the figure is on that square. After a student has taken a turn, he or she may elect to guess what the figure is and, if the student is correct, the game is over. If the student is wrong, he or she is out of the game and play proceeds.

When the game has been won, ask students to answer four questions in their journals.

1. Were you able to figure out the correct answer before all the squares were filled in?

2. As you played the game, what went through your mind as you decided whether to

take the chance of identifying the figure, knowing that an error would put you out of the game?

3. If it had been your turn, would you have been confident enough to guess before the figure was complete?

4. What does the game suggest about how people can make decisions even before they can prove that decision is the correct one?

Arguing Inductively

Discuss

1. Define inductive reasoning . . . it is used.

Inductive reasoning consists of examining available evidence in the form of facts and examples, considering that evidence as representative of the whole, and generalizing that the whole would be a continuation of the sample.

2. What is the inductive leap?

The inductive leap is the decision that you have examined enough evidence to safely conclude that additional examination would yield identical results.

3. In what sense . . . process of reasoning?

Because the inductive leap skips over any remaining evidence, there is always the chance of error. The mental leap from examining your sample to assuming the sample represents all others of its kind could always leave an exception.

4. Why is inductive . . . possibility of error?

If inductive reasoning is not used:

a. person must examine every piece of evidence before reaching a conclusion, which is often neither practical nor possible.

b. person will gain nothing from experience and learn nothing from the information available.

Act

Choose two of . . . make your point convincing?

Have students brainstorm sources of evidence in small groups. The evidence should be readily available and directly related to the topic. For instance, if a student chooses number 4, "Excessive absence seriously affects a student's performance in class," he or she might say, "I would ask several teachers to look in their grade books and attendance books to see what kind of attendance their top five students had last semester, and what kind of attendance their lowest five students had last semester."

For Your Journal

Saturday morning cartoons . . . you get it?

This journal topic is intended to start students thinking about the problems of gathering suitable evidence to study a question. When your students are finished, you might ask, "What ideas did you come up with for finding information? Where would you learn if children understand advertising that is directed at them?"

Reliability of Inductive Reasoning

Discuss

1. Assuming that you . . . affect your writing?

   Even though you would not deliberately lie, you must be scrupulous about accuracy. You must be certain of your facts. It is also a good idea to identify sources.

2. How can a writer . . . evidence is impartial?

   The writer must be careful not to fall into the trap of noticing only information that supports his or her tentative thesis. It's easy to overlook facts that contradict your opinion.

3. Explain the two . . . of the whole population.

   The preferred method is to carefully select a representative sample, being certain to include a broad cross-section of the whole.

   If it is impossible to control the sample well enough to be sure you have a cross-section, choose the sample randomly, entirely by chance.

4. Explain the importance . . . and your conclusion.

   If you do not show a direct connection between your evidence and your conclusion, the likelihood of error is high. As with the example of the news story given in the text, the writer should ask, "Is another conclusion possible?"

5. Name and explain . . . sample must be.

   a. The larger the population, the larger the sample you must examine.

   b. The smaller the population, the larger the percentage of the population you must examine.

   You might create another example of how these rules work by asking the class three questions:

   a. If you wanted to estimate what percentage of *students in the school* have cars, what is the minimum number of students you would question?

   b. If you wanted to estimate what percentage of *seniors* have cars, what is the minimum number of seniors you would question?

   c. If you wanted to estimate what percentage of *students in this class* have cars, what is the minimum number of students you would question?

Act

Each of the . . . explain the problem.

   Tell students to apply the five rules of inductive reasoning to each of the generalizations. Since each of the generalizations could have multiple weaknesses, one sample correct answer is provided for each.

1. Is the evidence true? The *National Tattler* is a tabloid whose reputation for accuracy is not high. Its publishers are sued several times a year. Very possibly the information is not true.

2. Is the evidence representative? If only the athletes were asked, that probably leaves a lot of students unrepresented.

3. Is the evidence representative? The students voting are the ones who found it convenient to attend meetings after school. The students the club wants to attract are not represented.

4. Was the evidence gathered impartially? Is it plentiful enough? This is one example and, assuming that this example may be true, it seems likely that the writer may be overlooking other evidence that doesn't seem to so perfectly support his or her contention.

5. Does the evidence support the conclusion? Silence does not necessarily equal great teaching. The class may be quiet because the students are all asleep. Or, for that matter, they may be terrified. Undoubtedly, there are many possibilities to explain the silence.

For Your Journal

Americans have been accused . . . this is the best.

While writing about something they would like to have allows students to dream a little, it also challenges them to show why this purchase is so special. Take time to ask students where they learned about the data, specifications, and characteristics of their dream purchase. How would this information stand up to the five guidelines for using inductive reasoning?

Gathering Your Own Evidence

Discuss

1. What is the thesis . . . well is it stated?
  The thesis of Jenni's essay, "This novel, *To Kill a Mockingbird*, helps describe the depth of the prejudice felt in those times by blacks and whites alike, and banning this book from the classroom would be hiding history and depriving students of some important lessons," clearly states the opinion that she will be supporting with evidence from the novel.

2. How does Jenni . . . gathering this information?
  Jenni has talked to several students about their reactions to the objectionable language. The approach is effective because she uses their comments to dispose of any fear that the cursing will harm students, and she explains how the racial insults function in the book. They reflect on, or characterize, the speakers, not the people being insulted.

3. How much detail . . . percentages were. Why not?

She provides very little information about the students she talked to. Telling exactly how many students she talked to and giving information about percentages are not necessary and would probably not be very interesting. She does edit their comments into some general attitudes toward the book, which seems appropriate for her purpose.

4. What point do . . . a separate paragraph? Why?

Both Mrs. Dubose and Bob Ewell provide lessons about people and the nature of prejudice. They were handled in the same paragraph because both illustrate the idea that the book has people doing unpleasant, and sometimes evil, things but those actions are presented in a context that makes their evil nature obvious. Mrs. Dubose and Bob Ewell could have been treated in separate paragraphs.

5. What is the purpose . . . and his children?

The paragraph about Atticus and his children makes the point that the book provides an example of how people should react when they encounter prejudice and injustice.

Act

Write an essay . . . for inductive reasoning.

Students should select a topic for which they can realistically expect to gather evidence. The five topics provided in the text have been selected because the information should be available, but students will have many more ideas.

As a first step, have your students write a plan that includes specific statements about where they intend to find needed information.

Chapter 10
Refutation

Instructional Objectives

As a result of having studied this chapter, students will

1. be able to define refutation

2. learn to analyze a writer's qualifications

3. learn to analyze a writer's evidence

4. learn to identify ten common fallacies

5. read and evaluate a refutation essay

6. write a refutation essay.

Vocabulary

Put the vocabulary words on the chalkboard and, if possible, leave them there for the duration of this chapter.

superficial	censure	submissive	indicative
judicious	paramount	stratagem	collaborate
precept	impinge	misconstrue	concord
vestige	innovation	candid	lucrative
dissension	absolve	coalesce	appall

Motivation

Several days before introducing this unit, tell students to begin reading the letters to the editor section of a local newspaper. They should watch for one or more letters expressing an opinion that they disagree with. Each student should clip his or her letter from the newspaper and tape the clipping to a sheet of lined notebook paper. On the designated day, students will bring their letters to class.

So that students will have an idea of what topics are represented, ask several of them to read their letters aloud. Then tell them to write answers to the following questions in the space below their letters. Each question should be answered as specifically as possible in a single sentence.

1. What do you suppose the writer looks like?

2. What kind of job do you think this person has?

3. How much education does he or she have?

4. What kind of family might this person come from?

5. Why does the writer feel this way?

6. Is this an opinion that people might take seriously?

7. Do you think this person is sincere?

8. Is the opinion based on fact or emotion?

9. What would be the best way to answer this opinion?

Some students will protest that there is no way to know the answer to several of the questions. They are correct, of course. "What do you suppose the writer looks like?", for instance, calls for some imagination.

Tell students that they are going to be studying methods of responding to other writers, and everything they can determine about the other writer will help that process. Even an imaginary picture of the other person will help the student decide how to handle his or her essay.

Then tell students to reread the letters and try to spot any clues that would help answer such questions as "How much education does he or she have?" or "Is the opinion based on fact or emotion?" When they have finished, they should have a reasonably accurate profile of the letter writer. If nothing else, they will be thinking about a real person instead of a faceless letter to the editor.

Examine Background and Evidence

Discuss

1. Why do so many . . . must be true?

Many people act as if the printed word were so special that untruths could not be published. They seem to think that errors are not allowed. This may come from the mistaken notion that anyone who can write for publication must be so special that his or her beliefs are not to be questioned.

2. How might a writer's . . . that person's opinion.

Everyone has personal circumstances that affect his or her view of a question. No one can be expected to be entirely objective. For instance, people's ages, locations, and relationships to the problem can all affect their viewpoints.

3. On what kind . . . have to be recent.

On some topics, facts that should or could affect your opinion are constantly changing. If technology is in any way involved, it's very possible that new evidence may come into being every day. For instance, the kinds of classroom uses for which computers are advantageous are not the same today as they were fifteen, ten, or even five years ago. In contrast, the evidence used to support a moral argument is not so likely to be affected by day-to-day changes.

4. How can you tell . . . to be convincing?

There is no specific rule dealing with minimum amounts of evidence. Complex questions call for complete, fully developed explanations and examples, but shorter papers need not be held to the same standards. If the writer has explained his or her idea so that the reader can understand, that is sufficient.

Act

Look through a number . . . feel as you do.

At the end of Chapter 10, students will be writing an essay in which they refute another writer's opinion. This activity is specific preparation for that essay, and a student's work here could be used for that assignment. The more difference of opinion students can find now, the more easily they will be able to handle the chapter's final assignment.

For Your Journal

Some incidents are . . . position perfectly clear.

This may be the one journal activity that a large number of your students want to keep private. They love to replay, with dramatic embellishment, recent discussions they've had with boyfriends or girlfriends, but this assignment offers an emotional release that surprises many student writers.

Others will produce humorous and satisfying methods of dealing with rude bureaucrats. Ask for volunteers to read, but don't press the issue if your students would rather keep this journal entry to themselves.

Examine the Logic

Discuss

1. What do all fallacies have in common?

All fallacious arguments have some flaw that makes the conclusion suspect.

2. Explain how an argument . . . conclusion is valid?

A conclusion can be true, even though the argument given is fallacious, if it is possible to reach the same conclusion through another, more logical, line of reasoning. To determine if the conclusion is valid, you must read the essay closely to see if additional, more valid evidence has been supplied.

3. At least half . . . example of each.

Fallacies that divert attention include: appeal to authority, appeal to ignorance, argument to the person, argument to pity, argument to popular attitudes, red herring, and the you-also fallacy. In many instances, even the faulty analogy could be viewed as an argument that takes the reader's attention from the issue being discussed.

4. One dictionary defines . . . using the word itself?

An argument that begs the question assumes what it attempts to prove in the same way that a circular definition repeats what it attempts to define. It supports an idea not by offering evidence but by repeating the idea. The repetition may be cloaked in a paraphrase, but it is a repetition, nonetheless.

5. In what way . . . analogies are faulty?

All analogies are comparisons, but they seldom, by their nature, offer proof of anything. They are useful in explaining ideas or in producing a mental picture, but analogies are perfect only if the two things being compared are identical. Any other analogy that is offered as evidence to support an idea is faulty. Since analogies are almost always imperfect and almost always presented as if they were evidence, in that sense they are all faulty.

Act

Name and explain . . . the following statements.

Some of the statements contain several fallacies, and some of the fallacies will overlap. One correct answer is supplied for each of the statements, but students should be encouraged to watch for additional possibilities.

1. Begging the question. The writer presumes that "peripheral vision is decreased, hearing is distorted, extreme heat causes fatigue, and additional wind resistance strains the rider's neck,'' when those are exactly the points that need to be settled before the safety of helmets can be proven or disproven.

2. False cause. The writer acts as if teenagers being on the street is a direct cause of crime. That cause-effect relationship has not been proven. Neither is there evidence to support the idea that creating a curfew will cause juvenile criminals to go home.

3. False cause. The writer presumes that the time relationship is a cause-effect relationship. There is no evidence presented that shows most marijuana smokers will graduate to cocaine.

4. Appeal to ignorance. The fact that no one has been able to put an end to the debate does not mean people should continue to smoke.

5. Argument to the person. The statement shifts the attention from the writer's need to lose weight to Dr. Geronoski's inability to follow his own advice. The doctor's problem does not change the writer's problem.

6. Begging the question. Whether the police are effective is the question at issue. The writer assumes what needs to be proven.

7. False analogy. The situation in the writer's neighborhood could not be identical to the international situation. The stakes are not the same; consequently, the analogy does not prove anything.

8. Argument to pity. Whether we feel sorry for the Exxon Corporation does not affect its responsibilities.

9. Begging the question. If the writer believes college is no more than a farm club for professional sports, that needs to be proven, not assumed without evidence.

Many people would disagree with the idea that college athletics have nothing to do with academics.

10. Begging the question. It has not been established that Beverly Cleary's books are "filthy."

11. Argument to popular attitudes. In the United States, and much of the world, the word *socialism* carries negative connotations. Attaching the term to Senator Clark's ideas makes him look bad without bothering to discuss the issue.

12. Red herring. The important issue here is what will benefit union members now, not the struggles of members from another era. The earlier struggles are an attention-getting, related topic, but they are not the topic of concern.

13. Appeal to ignorance. The fact that no one has proven astrology false does not prove it is true. If Marcy wants you to believe in astrology, it is her responsibility to supply evidence, not your responsibility to discredit her.

14. Appeal to authority. Nutrition and athletics are not the same thing. The athlete may be an expert in one area, but that does not mean he or she is trained in nutritional matters.

15. You also. A variation on the argument to the person, this statement tries to show that Jim's parents are acting hypocritically by drinking alcohol. They may be, but that does not mean they are wrong in their concern about other drugs.

For Your Journal

Sophists were ancient . . . you are using.

Students should have fun with this journal entry. Some will produce foolish, but humorous, arguments. Others may write very convincing arguments.

You may want to use this as a reinforcement activity. Some students will want to read their journal entries. Challenge the rest of the class to identify the fallacies being used.

Structure Your Refutation

Discuss

1. How is the audience . . . Explain fully.

The author of a refutation essay cannot count on the audience being friendly. The people you need to reach disagree with you and must be persuaded as carefully as possible. They are the same readers who have been taken in by the first writer's misleading arguments. You are not reinforcing an idea they already accept; you are trying to change their minds.

2. What is the thesis . . . of this difference?

"Mr. Williams's essay, while I'm sure it was well intentioned, was flawed by his own narrow point of view, atypical quotes, and several instances of fallacious reasoning."

This thesis has two parts: a concession to Mr. Williams and an assertion of Joseph's ideas. The concession statement is intended to establish Joseph as a reasonable person who tries to see both sides of an argument.

3. What are Joseph . . . they be improved?

Supporting point 1: "Mr. Williams is not a disinterested party who can be expected to have a balanced view of the situation."

Supporting point 2: "Mr. Williams also quotes several people whose opinions could have been predicted if he had identified them fully."

Supporting point 3: "Mr. Williams's third authority is even less appropriate."

Supporting point 4: "The use of an inappropriate authority was not the only fallacy contained in the essay."

Joseph's supporting points are clear, but students may have suggestions for additional ways to express the ideas. Encourage students to be as specific as possible. Concentrate on what improvement can be made, not what seems unsatisfactory.

4. Analyze paragraphs two . . . would you suggest?

Point out that Joseph refers to specific portions of Mr. Williams's essay and states precisely what his objections are. He uses quotes when necessary and explains himself fully. Perhaps just as important, Joseph is polite but firm. Again, insist that suggestions be specific.

5. How good are . . . conclusion? Explain.

The introduction brings up the topic in a natural-sounding manner; identifies it specifically by topic and author; and uses a strong, clear, two-part thesis. A title, which might have been helpful, is not mentioned.

The conclusion sums up the writer's point without resorting to a long list of supporting points. Altogether, both introduction and conclusion seem effective.

Act

Write a refutation essay . . . his or her opinion."

If students have trouble locating an essay with which they strongly disagree, have them use several essays dealing with the same topic. They need only refute one or two arguments in each essay. Students who use this option should completely outline each of the essays they will use. Have them use the same format given earlier in this chapter— list the thesis of each article and the opinions with which they disagree.

When students write the refutation essay, they will need to use a thesis sentence that shows what all the articles have in common. "Several writers seem to base their opinions about capital punishment for juveniles on inadequate and outdated evidence." As they refute each opinion one at a time, they should identify each article and author, and tell where they saw the article.

Chapter 11
The Research Paper

Instructional Objectives

As a result of having studied this chapter, students will

1. focus appropriately on a research topic

2. write a preliminary research outline

3. gather resources using a research checklist, facilities available in the library, and a working bibliography

4. take clear, concise, accurate notes

5. organize and write a first draft from their notes

6. learn to revise research papers in several distinct steps

7. learn three methods of documenting sources

8. read and evaluate a research paper

9. write a research paper with correct documentation.

Vocabulary

Put the vocabulary words on the chalkboard and, if possible, leave them there for the duration of this chapter.

facetious	schism	connotation	erudite
inveterate	auspicious	trenchant	relevant
finite	specious	recalcitrant	altruistic
shibboleth	alacrity	histrionic	placate
elucidate	cognizant	animosity	indubitable

Motivation

Ideally, a research project should be divided into several distinct steps. Students will be most successful with the unit if they know well ahead of time when various parts of the assignment will be due.

On the first day of the research paper unit, hand students a schedule of due dates, such as the following. Adjust the schedule to fit the number of class days you will devote to the unit. Tell students that a part of their final grade will come from each of the preliminary assignments. All starred assignments could be graded.

Day 1   Begin research paper unit.
    2   Select topic and turn in preliminary outline.*
    3   Start gathering resources.
    4   Turn in research checklist when complete.*
    5   Show teacher working bibliography.*
    6, 7   Read and take notes.
    8   Have note cards available to show teacher.*
    9, 10   Write the first draft.
    11   First draft should be complete.*
    12, 13   Revise first draft. Work with other students.
    14   Prepare the final copy.
    16   Last day to assemble paper and correct all errors.*

Focusing on a Subject

Discuss

1. Name and explain . . . the research process.

Selecting a topic is one of the most important steps in the research process because a mistake at this point could leave students looking for information that isn't very abundant or doesn't exist. Also, students will be working with the topic for several weeks and should carefully select a topic they want to learn about in detail. A third possible reason is the fact that students don't often get to select the areas of study within a course.

2. The text described . . . get some ideas?

Students should be able to suggest many sources but, if they have trouble starting, you might help by mentioning hobbies, parents, reading, friends, and career interests.

3. Describe the form of a preliminary outline.

The preliminary outline doesn't need detail. It consists of questions the student would like to see answered in the research paper. Introduction and conclusion are not necessary at this time.

4. What is the purpose of the preliminary outline?

When research begins, the preliminary outline should help distinguish between what is useful and what is not. It also helps to clarify the purpose of the research paper by forcing the student to put into words exactly what he or she is looking for.

5. How could a . . . is too broad?

When the topic is still vague and exists only in the student's mind, it is easy to overlook such problems as an overly broad topic. Seeing the parts of the topic in writing makes the problem obvious.

Act

Carefully select a . . . tentative outline prepared.

Students should have at least a weekend to consider research topics. If possible, get them thinking about the selection a week or two in advance.

Students do not always recognize the importance of a preliminary outline and may delay completing it. This is probably a good time to impress upon them the point that each step in the research process will affect final grades.

Gathering Resources

Discuss

1. Why is it important . . . for your topic?

Information can normally be found under not one but several headings. It is very possible that much valuable information might be found under a term that is slightly different from but closely related to the main topic.

2. What is a research checklist?

Information will probably be gathered from several sources in the library. The research checklist is a list of all the sources that contain material of use to the writer. It includes, but may not be limited to, the card or online catalog, *Readers' Guide to Periodical Literature,* pamphlet file, and any available special encyclopedias.

3. How would online . . . more recent information?

Online computer searches give access to such research aids as *Magazine Index,* which is updated daily. Compact discs are usually updated monthly so they are not as current as the online search, but they are so much more compact and easy to use than the *Readers' Guide* that students seem to be more successful in finding information.

4. What is a working bibliography? . . . a spiral notebook?

The working bibliography is a list of sources. Each source, with its essential bibliographic information, is written on an index card. These cards can then be arranged in whatever order is appropriate for the various steps in the writing process.

5. Describe the content . . . for a magazine?

The bibliography card for a book contains the author's full name, the book's title (underlined, and including subtitle), the city of publication, the publisher's name, and the year published. The bibliography card for a magazine article contains the author's full name, the full title of the article (in quotation marks), the title of the periodical (underlined), the date of publication, and the page numbers of the article.

Act

It's time to . . . you need to read.

Allow an appropriate amount of time for gathering materials. Students should have in hand as many of their books and articles as possible before starting to read.

Remind students that they may have to adjust their plans if some material they wanted was not available. Also, they may have found information that suggests new ideas they would like to investigate. If any changes are likely, they should update their tentative outlines.

Reading and Taking Notes

Discuss

1. List three reasons . . . for taking notes.

With index cards, students can sort according to author, subtopic, or source. They can put the cards in chronological order, or in the sequence to be used for the final paper. The cards can be used to compose the final paper by experimenting with different organizational patterns. If new information is found, it can be filed with the old cards without having to rewrite anything. Finally, information that turns out to be of little use can easily be set aside.

2. Name the three pieces . . . each of them?

Besides the note itself, each note card should include a meaningful heading, the author's last name, and specific page numbers. The heading will correspond to the major headings in the outline and will help organize information. Also, headings will help locate cards during the research process.

The author's last name establishes a connection with the working bibliography. When students document sources, all the necessary information will be available on the corresponding bibliography card.

The page number will be necessary for final documentation and is the one piece of information that cannot be included on the bibliography card.

3. List the three kinds . . . might be appropriate.

The three kinds of notes are summary, paraphrase, and direct quotation. The summary makes it possible to include a lot of information in a small space. The paraphrase gives a more detailed record in the student's own words.

Direct quotes are appropriate in three situations: if the original would be shorter than a paraphrase, if paraphrasing would take all the color out of the message, or if a paraphrase might not be as accurate.

Act

Begin taking notes . . . not to use it.

Impress upon students that they will benefit from an abundance of notes. Take time to work with individuals until you can see that they have a sense of what will be useful and what will not.

Writing the First Draft

Discuss

1. What is the purpose . . . by their headings?

The note card headings correspond to the student's tentative outline. If there is a problem with having enough information for some part of the research paper, it will become apparent at this point.

2. Besides organizing the . . . starting to write?

Besides establishing a basic organization, sorting the cards by their headings makes it possible to see what kinds of natural groupings might exist. It is also possible that a few cards might not seem to fit in anywhere. These can be saved for possible use later, or the student may need to look for additional information.

3. In what way is the outline still tentative?

In the process of writing a first draft, new relationships or new ways to include interesting facts may become apparent. The outline is a flexible guide for times when the writer needs help. It is not a straitjacket.

Act

Following the steps . . . or changes later.

This is a good time to leave the students to their work so that they can get information down on paper as quickly as possible.

Revising the First Draft

Discuss

1. What is the advantage . . . before revising it?

Some time away from the research paper between the writing and revising steps will help the student be more objective.

2. Why is it unwise . . . several small steps?

Revising the paper in several small steps makes it possible for the student to devote attention to one aspect of the paper at a time.

Act

Go back to . . . area of improvement.

This is an ideal time for students to help each other. Allow time for them to exchange drafts with a number of other students and go through the same four revision steps.

Preparing the Final Copy

Discuss

1. What is the difference . . . disadvantages of each.

Footnotes supply complete bibliographic information at the bottom of a page. Endnotes take the same form as footnotes except that they are typed on a separate sheet at the end of the paper.

Footnotes are harder to type because the student must allow enough room for them at the end of each page, but they are easier for the reader to use. Endnotes are easier to type, but result in more page turning for the reader.

2. Describe parenthetical documentation . . . and reader?

Parenthetical, or internal, documentation is inserted into the text and directs the reader to the books and magazines listed at the end of the paper. Since complete bibliographic information is given at the end of the paper, the parentheses contain only the minimum information needed to identify the source. Internal documentation is more informative than endnotes because it provides the author's name and a page number within the text. Endnotes supply only a number to direct the reader to the end of the paper. Parenthetical documentation is less informative than footnotes because the footnote would have all the bibliographic information available at the bottom of the page.

Act

Prepare the final . . . your teacher's directions.

Students should use the model research paper as a guide for their final copy. If you prefer either footnotes or end notes to parenthetical documentation, explain the choice to students and use the model paper to show what adjustments should be made. Although parenthetical documentation is now the MLA standard, some colleges have not yet made the change, and you will want students to be prepared for variations in style.